ON THE LOOSE

John Button

John Button was leader of the government in the Senate and industry minister from 1983 to 1993. He is a professorial fellow at Monash University and a frequent contributor to magazines and newspapers. He has travelled extensively.

BY THE SAME AUTHOR

Look Here (editor)

Flying the Kite: Travels of an Australian Politician

ON THE LOOSE

John Button

THE TEXT PUBLISHING COMPANY
MELBOURNE AUSTRALIA

The Text Publishing Company
171 La Trobe Street
Melbourne Victoria 3000

First published 1996

Typeset by Midland Typesetters
in Bembo 11/13
Printed and bound by
McPherson's Printing Group
Designed by World of Wonders

National Library of Australia
Cataloguing-in-Publication data:

Button, John, 1933– .
On the loose.

ISBN 1 875 847 35 9.

1. Button, John, 1933 – Journeys.
2. Travel – Humour. I. Title.

910.4

Many of the pieces in this book first appeared in different form in the *Age* and the *Sydney Morning Herald*.

Contents

High Days and Holidays

Modern Life

Letters from the Fringe

Talking Politics

Postcards

Afterlife

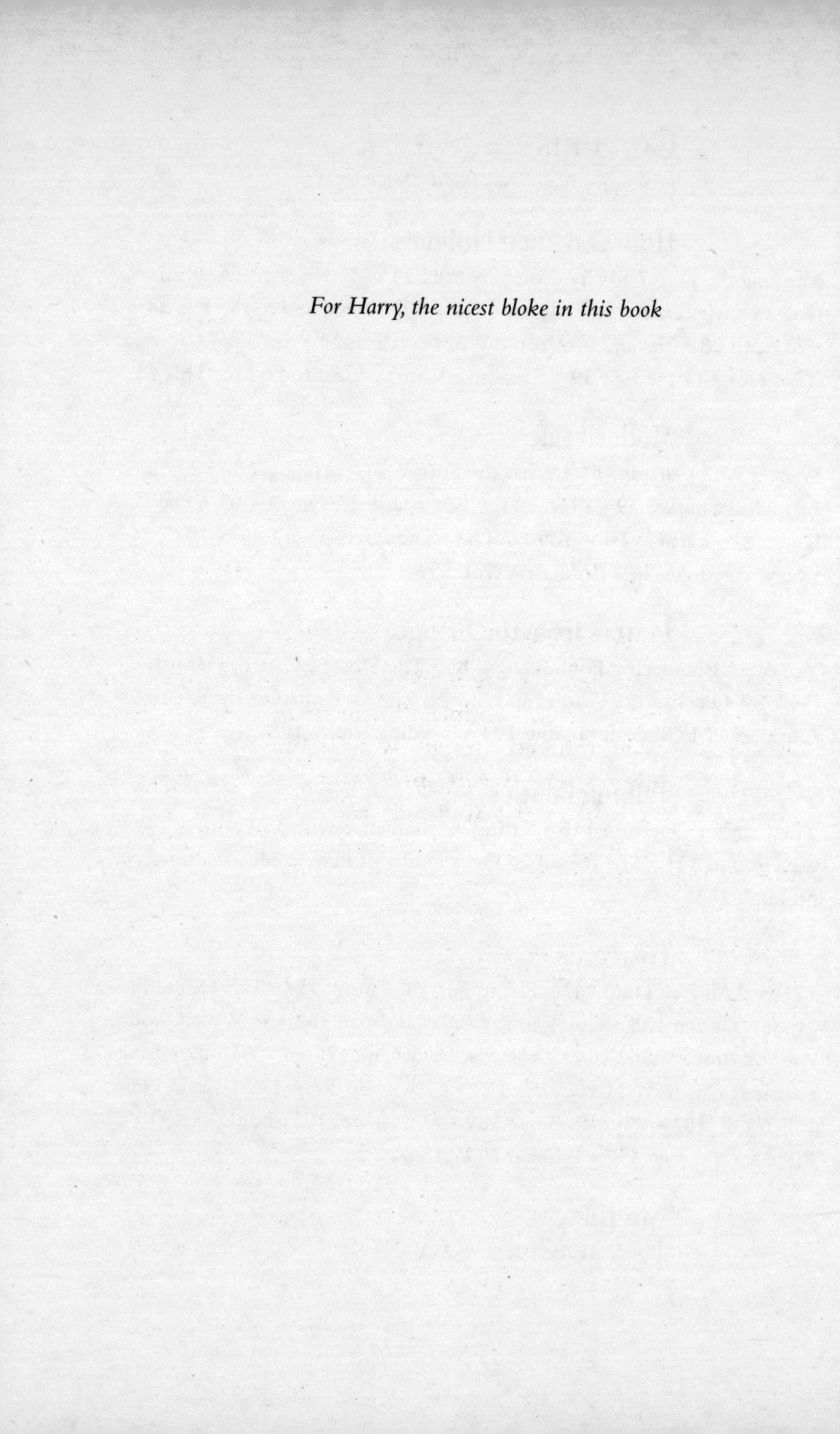

For Harry, the nicest bloke in this book

Prologue: *Non Sono Piu un Senatore*

I DELIVERED my letter of resignation to the president of the Senate. It was short and simple. 'Pursuant to Section 19 of the Constitution I hereby resign as a Senator for the State of Victoria.' From behind a big mahogany desk the president glanced at a clock on the wall and said, '10.12 a.m. on 31 March 1993.' Then he opened a large leather-bound book and started to write. He could talk and write at the same time. An enthusiastic international traveller, he began to tell me about a trip he proposed to make before his own impending retirement. I didn't recognise the name of the country. I guessed it was in Africa.

Africa seemed remote. I was contemplating my own uncertain future. Watching the president writing in the leather-bound book I imagined that this is what a mortuary attendant does when he signs you in, or St Peter before he ushers you through the pearly gates of the private sector. The images seemed at the outer limits of gloom or euphoria. Perhaps, I thought, he's a prison governor, signing me out after eighteen years: no remission for good conduct.

An hour later at the airport I said goodbye to my commonwealth driver whose passenger I had been for fifteen years since I became deputy leader in the Senate: probably my best friend in Canberra.

I was never entirely comfortable with the Canberra thing. For newcomers to national politics the Sunday night flight to the capital is a date with destiny, a ticket to where it all happens. As time passes, things change. You present your ticket to the flight attendant with the heavy heart of an inmate returning to a lunatic asylum after weekend release.

The physical isolation of the national parliament is all-pervasive. Shortly after I was first elected I remember going one Friday evening into a gift shop in a Melbourne suburb. As the shop assistant wrapped my parcel I said to her, 'It's very nice to be in a shop.' She gave me a startled look. I felt I should explain. 'You see,' I said, 'I've been in Canberra for a month.' She looked even more startled and glanced at the telephone on the counter. I paid my money and left quickly.

It's not, of course, as if Canberra has no shops. It's just that Parliament House, surrounded by ring roads and acres of necropolis lawns, is so remote from them. Like workers on an oil rig, parliamentarians are essentially confined to their own society: the people who work in the structure. The commerce of the streets, chance urban encounters of a third kind, are rarely experienced.

Back in Melbourne after resigning, I decided that my change in lifestyle warranted some overdue running repairs. Briefly contemplating a psychiatrist, I finally opted for the doctor, the optometrist and the dentist. My doctor said there was nothing wrong with me. I felt slightly miffed, but grateful for Medicare—paying cash for that advice would have seemed extravagant. At the optometrist I lay back and thought of England while stinging drops were put in my eyes. Not much wrong there either. The dentist's practice was located in a logistically inconvenient outer suburb, requiring unaccustomed use of the street directory and a parking meter. He removed two broken-down—but cosmetically important—teeth and told me to come back in two hours' time.

I decided to explore the local shopping centre . . . getting back in touch as it were. It turned out to be a mistake. It was hot and school holidays. I had a briefcase in one hand and held a handkerchief over my mouth with the other, so as not to frighten the children. I realised later that I probably looked like a deranged bank robber. Sadly some people recognised me. I imagined them muttering, 'He's gone down hill since he left politics.'

It was lunchtime, and I couldn't eat. Sufficient excuse to indulge myself with a malted milk. I plunged into a milk bar which seemed to be a meeting place for the local Italian community. Spotting me from behind the espresso machine the proprietor shouted, '*Senatore, buongiorno*.' He turned to a group of men playing cards at the back of the shop. '*E Senatore Button*,' he announced.

Feeling an explanation was in order, I tried to say, '*Non sono piu un senatore*,' but the two 's' sounds were too much. All that emerged was a sound like a whistling kettle. Maybe, I thought afterwards, the mixture of speech and sound effects might have roughly translated as 'I'm not a whistling kettle any more', a roundabout way of saying, 'I've retired from politics.' I lapsed into sign language and the proprietor busied himself with the malted milk. The card players looked at me as if I were a deranged bank robber, shrugged philosophically and resumed their game.

I went into a huge shopping mall. It was like Dante's Inferno. Music blared from loudspeakers, mums sat drinking at an outdoor bistro set in a plastic rainforest, and kids zapped up and down on skateboards. In an electronics shop I tried to engage the attention of a multicultural and adolescent shop assistant who was picking his teeth and fiddling with the volume controls on a ghetto blaster. I finally purchased a nine dollar cassette tape.

'What's your name and address?' he demanded.

'What's that got to do with you?' I whistled at him from behind my handkerchief.

'Company policy,' he replied with a patronising stare.

For a moment I contemplated an argument. There seemed to be a civil liberties issue at stake. On second thoughts, I decided I was in no shape to fight it.

A few days later I walked out the front gate of my house with a briefcase in my hand on my way to a temporary office in the city. There was no car waiting for me so I walked up the hill and caught the tram just as I used to do eighteen years before. In the office there were fourteen messages on the answering machine. I wrote them all down in longhand and began to ring back. Two of them were crackpot inventors, two were unemployed scientists who thought I might be able to find them a job, and one was a retired businessman who thought I might like a chat about the state of the country. 'Not my problem,' I felt like saying. '*Non sono piu un senatore.*' I thanked God for secretaries who'd handled these sorts of calls when I was a minister. Forgive me, for I knew not what you did. Then someone arrived with a bunch of flowers with a card which said, 'Welcome back to the real world.' I knew at once that it was from my wife. You see, she thought it was all rather funny. She'd met a lot of politicians over the years. In her view, they were all a bit out of touch.

High Days and Holidays

Minding the Dog

AFTER THE Christmas festivities were over, I waved goodbye to them at the front gate. 'Have a good time,' I said. 'And don't worry about anything here.' I went inside and found a note on the kitchen table. It was pretty straightforward. 'Don't forget to feed the dog. PS: Eat properly yourself.' The postscript I understood. They'd seen me coming back from the corner store with four tins of camp pie in a string bag. Camp pie, they thought, was a legacy of my primitive childhood. But as if I'd forget the dog? A few days later I received a fax: 'Please make sure the automatic sprinkler system is working.' Once again it seemed straightforward: not a problem.

In fact I'd worked out in my own mind quite a complex and exciting map of how I'd spend my time alone. I would confirm my frequent assertion that Melbourne's a great place to be at holiday time. I'd work for an hour or so each day, read some Christmas books on a banana lounge in the sun, make some running repairs around the house, see a film or two in the evenings, clean up the garden, watch some videos of missed movies, and perhaps drop in on the cricket. As it turned out there was no sun, almost no cricket, and for serious gardening you needed a wetsuit and flippers. But I was prepared for everything else. I even asked, before they left, for written instructions on how to work the video. I was eager with anticipation. Things like feeding the dog, shopping, and keeping an eye on the sprinkler system would fit well into the schedule.

The dog, I decided, would eat properly. Every second morning I made a list and went shopping. I came back with the things I'd ticked off the list: three bananas, two apples, four apricots, a smoked cod, milk, bread, and the dog's meat. It was good quality dog's meat: chopped up beef or horse, and bones with big round ball joints like Henry VIII used to chew on. 'Anything else?' the girl in the butcher's shop would ask.

'No, just dog's meat,' I'd say. She looked at me sympathetically. She thought I was eating it myself. I expected the dog to be pleased. In fact, our relationship deteriorated.

It started to bark at every sound, even the distant rumble of a train. It imagined it was sharing the management responsibility. Every afternoon, from lunchtime to dusk, the dog sat staring at me through the glass back door. It became unnerving. 'Go away,' I'd shout. Then the dog would cock its head on one side—'prettily,' the family would say—and go on staring with sad, moist eyes, clouded with sentiment. I could hardly wait for it to get dark.

The sprinkler system was a different problem. I'd long suspected it behaved erratically. This summer it rained so much in Melbourne, and the ground was so wet that I couldn't tell if it was working or not. I had to see it in operation. So I'd creep out at night with a torch, trying to catch the sprinkler in action, searching around like a modern-day Sherlock Holmes. In the daytime I stood in the garden with an umbrella waiting for it to work. All the water seemed to be coming from above: Melbourne's big sprinkler system in the sky. I sent off a fax. 'Sprinkler system working, but totally uncompetitive.'

So much for the request items. There were plenty of other things to be done . . . washing, ironing, painting, fixing up this and that. People asked me out for evening meals. At dinner on New Year's Eve there was a woman guest who seemed to know a lot about food and wine. She worked in a restaurant. 'What do you cook when you're on your own?' she asked. It was clearly not the time to mention camp pie.

'I eat quite a lot of smoked cod,' I whispered confidentially. 'Lightly poached and served with a white sauce.'

She giggled loudly. 'This man,' she announced, 'makes that awful white sauce we used to get at school. With parsley,' she added.

Mortified, I said nothing. But I appreciated the tip and added parsley the following day.

I began studying cooking books to improve my repertoire. They seemed very complex. Grams and milligrams of this and that: strange ingredients. It was all too extravagant for one person. Parsley in white sauce represented sufficient progress.

I ticked off some of the movies in the entertainment guide. I went to *Hard Rock West* twice in a week. I became fascinated by Dennis Hopper and his maniacal stare. I thought he's the man to come around and fix the dog. Or, perhaps, if I could learn to imitate him, the dog would stop staring at me.

At the video shop I fell for the special: take five for a week and save five dollars. I took five home and put them on the kitchen table. They began to weigh on my mind. What if I wasted the five dollars I'd saved? Jack Nicholson, Humphrey Bogart and Clint Eastwood stared at me reproachfully from the covers. They began to look like the dog. I gave in.

'You look tired,' someone said. 'Living it up last night?'

'No,' I replied sheepishly, 'watching videos.'

If I went out in the evening, I'd say at 10 p.m., 'I have to go home now.'

'You're on holiday,' people would reply. 'There's no hurry.'

'I'm sorry, I just have something urgent to do before tomorrow.' In retrospect it seemed rude. In fact, it's a condition—like bronchitis, or paranoia.

On the evening prior to New Year's Eve, I carried the rubbish bin out to the front gate. I looked up and down the street. I could only see three rubbish bins on the footpath. Usually there's a long line of them, standing, one or two at each gate, in lurid colours, like old-style hookers. 'Must have changed the collection night,' I thought. I picked the rubbish bin up and carried it inside again.

The next morning I heard the garbage truck go past as usual. Then I worked out why there were so few bins. Everyone was away. They were all on holiday. I was home alone. By default, I was the neighbourhood watch.

In reality, I couldn't claim to be the neighbourhood watch. We have one of them already. He lives down the street, and he never goes away. He knows everything. He's fascinated by security and the police: perhaps, I think, a legacy of an East European past. The other day he showed me an expired credit card he'd picked up in the street. He had a feeling it belonged to someone who'd been murdered in Sydney. He was taking it to the police station.

And there's Bob. He's eighty and as fit as a fiddle. He walks up and down the street each day, and he doesn't go on holidays either. He's been on the same page of the street directory all his life. He knows what goes on too, but he keeps it to himself. 'Come on the Cats,' he shouted at me across the street on New Year's Day—and he's an Essendon supporter.

They're all coming back from their holidays now, complaining about the weather. The bins will all be out tomorrow night. They say there's nothing much to do at the beach when it's wet. There's been plenty to do here, and a lot of it has been done. I developed new competencies. In fact, passing the newsagent the other day, I thought I might put a notice in the window:

DISCREET HOME SERVICES

Washing taken in, ironing (handkerchiefs only), house cleaning, odd jobs, casual cooking (light meals), gardening (weather permitting), watering, video advisory service. NO DOG MINDING.

Apply . . .

Why Bloody Australia Day?

I conducted a small survey of my own. I asked people what Australia Day commemorated.

The Lebanese milk bar proprietor look at me suspiciously. 'What you want to know for?' he asked. Then he said it was a day when people had a holiday, but 'I gotta bloody work'. He turned the question back at me, like Joh Bjelke-Petersen answering a reporter. 'Why bloody Australia Day? Anzac Day, I know why. But why Australia Day?'

A Greek woman said it was a day which celebrated less work. Another woman corrected her. 'That's Labour Day. Australia Day is the day Captain Cook discovered Australia.' I asked a senior, well-educated public servant. There was a pause. 'I haven't a clue,' he said. 'That means my family doesn't know either.' A teenage girl hesitated before deciding it meant 'the day the Queen took over Australia'. Several people thought it commemorated the federation of the states.

I told Bob, the wise old pensioner who lives in my street, what people understood about Australia Day. 'Well,' he said, 'that's typical. They think they know everything these days but they know sweet FA.' I asked him. He said it was the day Australia became a nation. He wasn't quite sure what that meant. A visitor from England, an Australian who has lived in London for years, got it wrong too. 'But it doesn't matter,' she said. 'Australia is marvellous. People overseas don't know how good it is.'

When Governor Phillip's fleet of eleven ships entered Sydney Harbour on 20 January 1788 he thought it 'the finest harbour in the world'. At Sydney Cove they raised the flag and took possession in the name of King George. The teenage girl was almost right.

They were tough times in 1788. In Phillip's first speech he told the convicts that men found in women's tents would be shot. Anyone who stole food would be hanged. He was a law-and-order man. Not many convicts thought Australia was marvellous. The Aborigines watched the arrival of the First Fleet with an anxiety which turned out to be well placed.

There's a case for saying Australia Day is really New Year's Day. January is a funny month. People are on holidays. They dribble back to work, but their minds are not so with it. Ambitions, new year aspirations and hard schedules remain in the in-tray until February. There are distracting relaxations. It's tempting to slip away for an hour or so to the cricket, the tennis or the beach. At home the television screens are cluttered with old soapies and B-grade movies. Addicted viewers think it's a good time to read books, borrow a video, eat out or go to a movie. If we do watch television it's out of curiosity, just to satisfy that part of us committed to catastrophe. January is the disaster month, when television brings images of catastrophe into every house: things like bushfires, earthquakes and Mr Bobbitt.

As the month progresses we start to see and read about the year ahead. There are previews and forecasts, even fleeting images of politics: man-made disasters some people would say. Parliament is about to resume. Politicians start limbering up. Aspiring and recycled statesmen appear briefly on TV, honing their images for the coming season. Yes, after Australia Day, the action really begins: in politics, business, work. We emerge from limbo into the new year.

In the front of my pocket diary there is a list of Australia's national public holidays. There are nine. Five of them are Christian festivals appropriately recognising the dominant religion of Australians. One, the Queen's Birthday, presumably symbolises 'the day the Queen took over Australia'. It falls in

June in all states except Western Australia, where it happens in October. Anzac Day falls on the same day everywhere. Generally people know what it's all about. There are additional holidays in each of the states: for Labour Day, a horse race, a regatta, or an agricultural show. Only Anzac Day and perhaps Australia Day have possible symbolic relevance for all Australians. The rest have significance for only a section of the community: primary producers, punters, unionists, bank workers and raving monarchists.

Yet my small survey about Australia Day sent people groping after images of what it means. This, I suspect, is uniquely Australian. I can't imagine an American who didn't know what the Fourth of July was about. The British understand the Queen's Birthday. It's pretty simple. It provides a focal point for history and tradition, and nostalgia for better times. In France they know about Bastille Day. In Asia, and on the subcontinent, independence days are meaningful events. Australians by contrast are careless and fickle about determining national priorities. A holiday is a holiday. It makes some sense when you think about it.

Australians are also bad at deciding what they should be anxious about. We even get anxious about the significance of public holidays. Anzac Day and Australia Day, for example, produce passing symptoms of anxiety. Experts sit in TV studio chairs like Rodin's *Thinker* and ponder what it all means to be Australian. 'Who am I,' they ask. 'Who are we? What is the answer? What is the question?' Are we too unpatriotic? Too lacking in the trappings of nationalism? Is this another January disaster?

The great British judge Lord Denning once sentenced a criminal to a period of imprisonment. 'There was a time,' he said, 'when we used to send our prisoners to Australia. I understand some of them did quite well out there.' For a long time we didn't like to be reminded of our beginnings. But that is what Australia Day is all about. Our beginnings. That's what it commemorates.

In 1788 the first dwelling was Governor Phillip's tent. His

subjects were variously described as 'the scum of the earth', 'half starved', 'debauched', 'rebellious' and 'pitiful'. They'd been sent to Australia because distance from European civilisation was both a punishment and a virtue. Perhaps we should remind ourselves about all that. The Lebanese milk bar proprietor, the Greek lady, old Bob, and the teenage girl should know about it. Then Australia Day might be a celebration of what Australia has become since then. We might think the place is not so bad after all.

Americans whoop it up on the Fourth of July. But intolerance, violence and social inequalities cloud the American dream. Britons celebrate their glorious past. Half the population wants to emigrate. A lot of the world's people would like to live here. That is no reason for complacency. We've plenty to do to improve our institutions, and to strengthen our sense of community. And Aboriginal reconciliation is recognising that Australia Day commemorates something which need not be a disaster for Aborigines forever.

If Australia Day is dragged out of the closet, Lord Denning's words make more sense. 'Some of them' and their descendants *have* done quite well out here. We're not lacking in defects and problems, but these things are relative. And relatively we are a tolerant, law-abiding, innovative and increasingly outward-looking society. That's something to celebrate: being 'a marvellous place'. Australia Day is a good day to do it.

The Year of the Dog

Sometimes people worry unnecessarily about things they don't understand. It seems silly. For example, I don't understand Chinese. But I once noticed a large banner hanging in front of the casino in Perth. It worried me. It said, as I recall it, '*kung hee fat choi*'. Clearly, it was a clumsy attempt at *goong hay fatt choy*, the Chinese New Year greeting. The spelling seemed wrong, but so what? It was a try, and for a minute or two I felt good about it. Western Australians were obviously tolerant, generous, moderately sophisticated and hospitable after all. Then I saw a group of Taiwanese tourists alighting from a crowded bus. They were being prized out like sardines from a can, by a man with a tickboard instead of a fork. As one would expect, the first of them came out easily: neat and shiny. The last two seemed broken and crumpled. They looked around for the rest of their group. Then they scuttled off under the banner, and into the casino. Happy New Year!

The banner I realised must be an English version of Mandarin: a Western Australian version perhaps. *Goong hay fatt choy* is Cantonese. It means, some say, 'Congratulations and gather your wealth'. Whatever it means in Mandarin, or Cantonese, a casino seemed a bad place to start. But Chinese like gambling and probably see it differently.

Certainly Chinese New Year is different. It's not just a one-day stand. It lasts a week, and has a long history and powerful traditions, derived from a rural culture in which animals and seasons are all-important. Much of the week is spent eating, and drinking, and giving presents. Married people give gifts to unmarried people. There is widespread giving of money in red envelopes. It's lucky money. During the Chinese New Year five dollar notes are hard to come by, because most of them are in red envelopes. Red envelopes that are kept for three years are said to bring better luck. By then, perhaps, another economic downturn will be over. Chinese restaurants will fill up again. There will be numerous banquets of many courses and plenty of toasts to a prosperous new year.

Watching all this, I've often wondered how much Chinese drink. It is hard to say because you don't see many drunk Chinese. Perhaps they're quiet achievers. Someone, I thought, should research it. I found a clue in the Museum of Chinese History where a book told me about the autopsies on Chinese who died in the Ballarat and Bendigo goldfields in the 1850s. There were lots of them. Quite a number died from 'inflammation of the liver', which sounds a bit suspicious. But times were different then. Today's Australian Chinese enjoy their new year festivities in plush restaurants which serve good wine.

At the end of January a Chinese friend told me he'd been to a dinner on Australia Day. To me it seemed an extravagant thing to do. But at Chinese New Year he goes out every night for a week. He helps with street processions, and takes kids to see the Chinese dragons. It is a busy time.

The Vietnamese have a similar new year tradition. Tet falls at the same time as the Chinese New Year. But they start letting off practice crackers in the middle of January. Like the Chinese they give presents and pay visits to relatives and friends. They buy new clothes. The new year represents a fresh start.

I have a sort of cantilevered calendar, with two New Years, one starting on 1 January, and the other on 10 February. My animal sign in the calendar suggested I was a dreamer with a thirst for knowledge. I began studying the sign and following its advice. It could be an interesting learning experience. A bit of luck thrown in would help. I'd kept the red envelopes with the lucky money over the years. Perhaps the Year of the Dog would be the lucky one.

Then a Melbourne Chinese friend wrote me a letter. It was a business letter which concluded with the following paragraph:

> According to Chinese fortune telling book, the Year of the Dog is very good year for those who were born in the Year of the Rooster. A lot of money coming in and a lot of romance but if you get involved with women, your luck becomes bad. Therefore don't touch bad women this year.

Before the letter came I'd started to get interested in the idea of New Year celebrations as a sort of progressive dinner party when one moved on from one cuisine to another, one culture to the next, all in the inner suburbs of Melbourne or Sydney. It was all part of the rich fabric of multiracial Australia. But I didn't know what to make of the letter.

The message was confusing and I'm always cautious about defying predictions and advice. In this case I had to interpret it all myself. As a result I tended to walk around with my eyes on the ground. I was looking out for banknotes and avoiding a possible glimpse of a bad woman. It didn't seem very romantic.

It may not, of course, be good for everyone, but an extended multicultural new year must be good for the economy. From Christmas to Easter there are sales and holidays and festivals and long weekends and people eating in restaurants, buying new clothes, circulating money and giving each other presents.

Tet and Chinese New Year involve a sizeable proportion of the urban population. I decided to ask one or two people what they thought—another little survey. I spied my doctor friend in a restaurant. He is a man renowned for his urbanity and astuteness, with a degree of erudition remarkable in the medical profession. He seemed an ideal subject. I approached him as he stood up and moved away from his table. 'Tell me,' I said, 'what do you think about the Year of the Dog?'

There was a brief silence. I thought I caught a flicker of doubt, perhaps terror, in his eyes. He gathered himself together. 'What an extraordinary question to ask someone on his way to pass water!' he said curtly. Then he walked away. I interpreted this as a negative or even hostile response.

I decided to ask my pensioner friend Bob. He's always sensible about things, although on this occasion I suspected I knew what he would say. I thought he'd pretend not to hear the question. He'd put his hand to his ear and say, 'You want a hair of the dog? I'll be in that. I'll see you down at the tavern in half an hour. It can be your shout.' But he didn't say anything like that at all. 'What do you think of the Year of the Dog?' I asked.

He scratched his head thoughtfully, 'No,' he said. 'I can't see it this year. The Cats possibly, or the Eagles. The Crows will be good. Maybe the Magpies. But the Doggies, I just can't see it this year.' Which reminded me: the seasons change, the months go by on all the calendars, and another Australian festival is about to begin.

Mrs Daicos and Me

In March the Melbourne summer turns gently into autumn. It's the sunniest month: warm and usually reliable. But the light is different, slowly softening and at night there's a hint of crispness. Once you could tell from the changing weather, in your bones as it were, when the football season was about to begin. Now summer games merge into winter ones. February and March are riots of sport. In February the cricket is still in full flood, ebbing out into March. Football creeps up on us in February with the pre-season competition. It's been happening in one guise or another since 1988.

The overlapping of these two games is more apparent since Australian cricket pulled itself out of the doldrums, becoming less dour, less predictable, more crowd-pleasing.

I remember, in the late eighties, a grumpy old bloke in a pub telling me he hadn't missed a Test match at the MCG for thirty-five years, but that he wouldn't be seen dead at the cricket any more. 'A lot of no-hopers . . . not enough overs in the game . . . no spin bowlers with any class . . . in fact no spin bowlers.' I was thirsty so I stayed there listening to him while he rambled on. And he kept calling me 'son', which did a lot for my morale. 'What about the World Series—the one-day games?' I asked.

'Might fool young people,' he said, 'but it's not real cricket . . . lollipop men playing tip and run. Remember tip and run? We used to drop the bloody bat and run like hell. They don't even drop their bats.'

This discussion prompted me to renew my antique interest in cricket and see for myself. I slipped into the Melbourne Cricket Ground late one afternoon in the dying hours of a Test.

It was, of course, a beautiful day, but there seemed to be fewer people there than a game between AFL sides at the bottom of the ladder under lights on a cold, wet Friday night at Waverley. Coincidentally I chose a seat in a section of the stand sparsely occupied by single men (like me) who stared intensely at the scoreboard as if they were waiting for something to happen. If we'd had mackintoshes we might have all been at a blue movie. This unhappy thought made me a bit jittery and I decided to go home.

Later that year I found myself watching the final of the World Series on TV. It was a confusing experience, even though the players had their names printed on the backs of their shirts. And it was not long before my theories about the Melbourne weather in the month of March were shattered. The second time I turned on the TV there were men with mops poking around on the wicket, and a man on a mobile roller who looked as if he was flattening out a giant pizza. Viewers were presented with special rules to deal with this difficult situation. The umpires were subject to 'in-depth' interviews so they could explain it all. The formula was complex. You divide this figure by that figure by that figure, take so much off for the rain, and there you have it. Nothing they said gave me a feeling of confidence. I'd always thought of cricket as a relaxing game, but even on the best of days the TV presentation is not easy. Graphs of run-rates, placements on the ground of scoring shots by successful batsmen, times taken per over, the weather map with a moving indicator, all made hard work of it. I longed for the football to begin. Lou Richards or Crackers Keenan would explain it all. They'd even tell you when the umpires were wrong, or the rules needed changing.

Australian cricket got out of the doldrums by finding some fine new batsmen, and at least one spin bowler of real class. They excited the spectators, and became role models for budding young cricketers. My grumpy old friend from the pub might even be going to Test matches again. Cricket has once more become an international game of real significance. As our summer recedes the Australian team heads off overseas for exciting competitions in strange venues. We follow its fortunes on television. The goal posts go up again at the MCG.

Through the summer there are snippets in newspapers about football. They pop up like messages in bottles, floating on a tide of news about cricket, tennis, and summer disasters. The seriously addicted grab at them with anxious hands. There's news of the draft, of recruits and club finances: portents for the future, requiring serious consideration. In March the football shows start up on television, talking heads with not much to talk about. Professional sports writers preview the season ahead, with a series of implausible predictions. But it's my friend Mrs Daicos who really confirms for me that the football season is about to begin.

These days I often have a cup of coffee at a small restaurant in the city. It's usually served by a likeable young woman. For most of the year she displays a droll Australian sense of humour. But she's a dyed-in-the-wool Collingwood supporter, and she knows I'm passionate about Geelong. She's a great fan of the legendary Collingwood player Peter Daicos. In March she starts to get agitated. She moves into psychological warfare mode. 'Try that,' she says as she plonks a cappuccino on the table in front of me. 'You might have a better day than Geelong had in their last Grand Final.' I remark on the size of the toasted sandwich. 'If you can't eat it,' she replies, 'stick it in your handbag.'

She's unrelenting. I sometimes think I should take my business elsewhere. But I'm long-suffering. It toughens you up for difficult matches in the months ahead. And I try to fight back. 'You're so one-eyed,' I said one day, 'that I'm going to call you "Collingwood" or "Magpie".'

She glared at me, hands on hips. 'If you want to call me anything,' she said, 'call me Mrs Daicos.' So Mrs Daicos she is.

The truth is Mrs Daicos interests me. I have a flickering knowledge of anthropology. Enough to know she's really tribal: probably worse than me. I wonder if she's about to become an extinct species. She may be young, but perhaps she belongs in the past. What if Collingwood was forced into a merger or lost its home at Victoria Park? I'd like to ask her those questions. But she might tip a hot cappuccino over my head.

Australian Rules Football looks robust these days. Games are well attended. There are clubs from five states. The surrounding culture is alive and well, in print, on radio and on TV. Yet in football circles there is constant talk of crisis. Club presidents and pundits talk like politicians in the week before an election. A number of clubs are struggling financially. Costs are rising. The game, like the country, is said to be living beyond its means. There has been consistent pressure for clubs to be abolished or merged in the 'interests of the long-term viability of the game'. Poorer clubs clamour for a greater share of the cake. The chief commissioner of the AFL admonishes critics for factual errors. The language and the posturing are very familiar. Football has developed its own politics. Soon someone will say, 'These are the mergers we had to have.'

Some sentimental traditionalist wrote, 'The rot began when South Melbourne moved to Sydney.' The rot is symbolised by people talking of football as if it were an accounting problem. Once it was just a game. Now it's much more complex. Football is big business. It's a national game, and its government, the AFL Commission, sees television as its major source of revenue. Venues, schedules, starting times are all adjusted to accommodate this. Viewers and ratings seem to count for more than people who go to the games. Alien ideas to cut costs and enhance revenue are floated in the media. The reserves grade could be abolished; there might be night games mid-week; what about a night Grand Final? There are suggestions of more rule changes, and intemperate signs of over-governance as more umpires clutter the grounds. The insidious video footage, complemented by trials in the media, has more authority than the umpires or the loyal spectators. The men and women in the glass boxes seem too remote from the men and the women standing in the outer.

The sports commentator Garry Linnell once wrote that 'slowly but inevitably the game is being dragged from its birthplace in the suburbs of Melbourne into the bright and glossy world of big business'. There are always casualties of change like this. People are left behind by events beyond their control. Football has plenty of those, because change cuts across a vivid history and powerful traditions. If I asked Mrs Daicos, who stands behind the Collingwood goals each week, what she thought about it all, I suspect she'd say, 'I don't care much so long as they leave the Magpies alone.' An equally passionate supporter of other struggling clubs would probably say much the same thing. It may be unrealistic, but it's very human. Like the conflicts between the National Trust and a developer, between the forest and the bulldozer, it's a conflict which is never satisfactorily resolved. It needs wise heads, good communication and sensible compromises.

The first games identifiable as Australian football were played in the late 1850s. The real competition between clubs got started in the 1890s. Football is older than the Australian commonwealth, radio, the Labor Party and motor cars, and has outlived George Burns. Some of its history is written and some is told by word of mouth. Historians, academics, dramatists and poets have written books, essays, plays and poems about it. Politicians descend on the North Melbourne Grand Final Breakfast like galahs on a wheat crop. The loyalties of football transcend political allegiances and class barriers. They're as old and as Australian as Ayers Rock.

Attempts have been made to export Australian Rules football. Exhibition games have been played in the United States, Canada, New Zealand and Japan, without arousing great interest. These places have their own agendas and rival products. In Japan in 1987 I watched Hawthorn and Carlton stage an exhibition game in a stadium on the outskirts of Tokyo. The Japanese called it Ozzy Ball. A commentator shouted excitedly through a loud speaker system. I think he was hoping for a melee like they have in the Japanese parliament. The small crowd seemed unmoved. Afterwards I drove back to Tokyo with the owner of a TV station. He'd won a bronze medal in the 1936 Olympics. He lectured me on the declining moral fibre of Japanese youth. He said they needed toughening up. Perhaps, he thought, Australian football might be the answer. I never met anyone else who agreed with him. I'm in favour of exports, but of wheat, automotives, software and ships: things like that. I'm not in favour of exporting football. Some things which we like and do well should be kept for us. It's bad enough having games and possible finals in Perth, Brisbane or Sydney. One in Los Angeles or Vancouver would be terrible. Mrs Daicos and I would be totally disoriented. Imagine what she'd do when she served a cup of coffee to a tourist from America. And there wouldn't be the same sense of anticipation, and hands-on involvement, leading up to the first round on the last weekend in March.

If I had any sense I'd give up morning coffee in the week before the first game. There's enough to worry about without Mrs Daicos. Some of my favourite players are getting on in years. Old legs. They must be 'a yard slower'. That's what the experts say, drawing on their own experience. But sometimes they're wrong. And they overlook the new recruits. You have to go and see for yourself.

Walking to the football ground you feel like part of an army of foot soldiers on the move, converging from all directions. You wonder where they've all been for the last six months. Some carry banners, others are wearing their regimental uniforms: beanies, scarves and football jumpers. Mostly they look like guerillas sensing a battle. At the gate the man in the blue dustjacket clips your ticket. It's the same guy who was there last year. He might have been there all summer. 'Howya reckon we'll go today?' he says with a twinkle in his eye—exactly the same question he asked at the last game the year before.

You climb the stairs to a seat in the stand. There are a lot of familiar faces. The umpires walk onto the ground. The crowd boos. Then the teams run on. The whistle blows and the game starts. It begins tentatively. The players and crowd are slowly warming up, the crowd wondering, hopeful, watching intensely. In a few minutes they reckon those old legs are still working. And there are some new young ones. The first goal is kicked by a recruit. He's skilful and very quick, exciting to watch. You settle back in your seat convinced for the next six months it's going to be a great season—more than just something to keep you off the streets on a wintry Saturday afternoon.

Round the Bend and in the Pits

Melbourne hosts another high-profile event in March: the Australian Grand Prix. For eleven years it was in Adelaide. Now it's in Melbourne, and likely to be for some years to come. It's part of the annual Formula One international motor-racing season; sixteen races in sixteen different countries. Adelaide, a stately and dignified aunty of a place, never seemed quite right for it. So a nifty businessman, popularly known by the military style title of 'Major Event', snaffled it for Melbourne. It means globalisation for petrol heads, 'putting Melbourne on the map' for politicians.

The move from Adelaide to Melbourne aroused some controversy. Not everyone thought it was a good idea. Residents of Albert Park, the inner Melbourne suburb, chosen as the venue, protested: rather like anyone would, faced with a freeway in their back garden. Comfortable middle-class citizens turned into urban radicals. Greens identified environmental issues. There were many demonstrations. One I went to, on a beautiful sunny day in autumn, attracted a large crowd. There were older people who'd become angry, family groups on push bikes, others sitting on rugs on the grass, eating picnic lunches. A nicer bunch of people would be difficult to assemble. Speakers harangued them about 'rights' and the importance of 'empowerment'. In the sun, and the picnic atmosphere, the jargon sounded harsh and manipulative. The protests continued. Barricades were put up and pulled down. Yellow ribbons were hung from trees and cars as symbols of dissent. The state sent in the troopers to deal with it all, like Governor Hotham at the Eureka Stockade. Protesters were arrested and taken to court. Some became local martyrs for a lost cause.

Some of my best friends are petrol heads. They've always had trouble trying to persuade me of the virtues of Formula One racing as a spectator sport. Nonetheless I went to the Melbourne Grand Prix as a guest, invited by someone who perhaps hoped for my conversion. It was another occasion: a major event. I was a victim of my own curiosity.

I'd been to Formula One races before, the first time in Adelaide at the first Australian Grand Prix. There was a dinner the night before the final race. The British driver Nigel Mansell entertained the guests, using a whiteboard to explain the challenges of the Adelaide track: what speed he'd be doing on particular sections, the gear changes he'd have to go through on the bends, the number of seconds he had to do it in, what the computer told him, and so on. It seemed fascinating: the interaction of men and machines, reflexes, carburettors, nerves and torque. The following day we assembled in a raised enclosure overlooking the start. It was how I imagined the members' enclosure at Ascot. Everyone was there: the prime minister, the leader of the opposition, state premiers, manufacturers of spark plugs, Prince Edward, tyre dealers, George Harrison, and assorted TV faces. At lunch George Harrison autographed my wife's copy of the menu. We exchanged a few words. Two places away from him, I felt in the presence of greatness. That was enough. The excursion had been worthwhile.

It was a hot day in Adelaide. The air was full of fumes, and dust, and anticipation. Good conditions for drinking. It numbs the senses except for hearing. When the race started I began to learn the difficult language of Grand Prix speak: conversation interruptus. The cars flashed past whining like giant dentists' drills. The art is to remember what point of a sentence you were at before you went temporarily deaf. A coherent discussion requires luck and good management. I left Adelaide, the festival city, feeling none the wiser.

My next Grand Prix was at Monte Carlo. I happened to be there on a boat in the harbour. Monte Carlo is the cultural capital of petrol heads, and going to the Grand Prix seemed a sensible thing to do. There wasn't much alternative. For a few days the whole town is taken over by the event. There's a festival atmosphere of friendly informality. I watched the race from the balcony of an eighth floor apartment directly above the start. From there you could see the straight, and the track winding up the side of a mountain overhanging the sea. There was a party going on in the apartment. Mostly the guests were French, with a few extras from Peter Stuyvesant ads thrown in. I was introduced to various guests. '*Il est Australien*.' They stared at me as if I was a deranged brother of Crocodile Dundee. Later a couple of Englishmen started a sweep. I drew Alain Prost, a much favoured driver. The French guests began to treat me with greater interest. '*L'Australien a choisi Alain Prost*,' they would say as if I had some particular insight like reading the ticket before I picked it out of the hat. Prost led for the first three laps. Things were looking good. Then he was flagged into the pits and penalised four laps for beating the starter's flag. '*C'est tres triste*?' a Frenchwoman said sympathetically. Prost resumed the race and drove like a madman. I felt proud of him, but it was another lost cause. Ayrton Senna won the race. Later I wandered through the streets of this charming little tax haven. There was a nice village atmosphere. Drivers and crew mingled with the crowd.

Arriving at the Melbourne Grand Prix seemed like dropping in on the English army the day before the Battle of Agincourt. Flags and pennants flew from a series of little white marquees. Laurence Olivier might have stepped out of any one of them to make a St Crispin's Day speech. Instead there were girls in mini-skirts selling guides, souvenirs and bric-a-brac. We had lunch on the first floor of a pavilion overlooking the pits. Strategically placed TV sets told us what was happening outside. Earplugs were provided. We were advised to go to the stand on the roof for a better view of the start. Experts said, 'It's the box seat.' Earplugs in for the noise, hats on for the hot sun. The race began. Thirty seconds later it stopped when a car flipped on the first bend and broke into bits. Nobody in the box seats could see the first bend. People removed their earplugs. 'What happened?' they asked. 'Has there been an accident? Will it start again?' Rumours abounded. We went downstairs to find out from the television sets, for a drink, and to rehearse some Grand Prix speak.

Two men with heads more fuddled with chardonnay than petrol and a young woman accosted me as I adjusted my earplugs for the restart. 'You've got to admit it's better than football,' one man shouted.

'No,' I shouted back, 'I like the football better.' The young woman looked down her nose and snorted like a duchess meeting her first peasant. 'I prefer horse-racing too,' I added mischievously. 'Horses aren't noisy.' She snorted again and marched off like Margaret Rutherford. I looked around at the people sitting round the room. They sipped drinks and nibbled at cheese and nuts. Mostly their eyes had glazed over. They looked distinctly bored. There was a bit of Grand Prix chitchat about who was there and who wasn't. Being there was clearly important. Time to go.

I set off across Albert Park towards St Kilda Road. The pontoon bridge over the lake wobbled and swayed as people walked across it. Some had difficulty keeping their feet. Everyone walked with the studied concentration of the seriously inebriated, shrieking like kids at Luna Park. Some thought it was the highlight of the day. On the other side of the lake a covered pedestrian bridge straddled the race track. The crowd pushed up the stairs like sheep in a race. A few steps behind us three young men began to chant, 'baa, baa, baa'. Other people on the bridge took up the refrain: 'baa, baa, baa'. We were in a crowd of people imitating sheep. A Japanese couple in front of us began to giggle. 'Sheeps,' the man said. 'Very funny.' This, I thought, has to be an Australian Grand Prix.

I caught a taxi at the Queens Road side of the park. Behind me I could hear the roar of the cars. The cab driver was an African. As I got in, a transport inspector was shouting at the driver through the window. 'I'm sick of you. I'm going to file a report. I'll throw the book at you.' I didn't like the tone of voice. This I thought is a bad incident, perhaps racist. Not the sort of thing which should be happening at the Australian Grand Prix. 'What's the trouble?' I asked the driver, who was nonchalantly chewing gum.

'The inspector,' he said coolly, 'thinks I should be wearing socks and shoes.'

'Well, it is pretty hot,' I said limply. In Domain Road I noticed a little Morris Oxford in the traffic ahead of us. It had yellow ribbons tied to the rear bumper bar. More yellow ribbons trailed from the rear windows. As we drew alongside I saw that there were two frail-looking old ladies in the car. They were wearing floral hats. I recognised them for what they were: urban radicals. On the back window of their car there was a sign saying, 'Grand Prix. Never Again.'

25 April

Passing pedestrians might have wondered what I was doing. I sat in the car for nearly an hour on Anzac Day morning. I was listening to the radio and I was a bit spellbound. A World War II digger was recounting how he escaped from the Germans in Crete, and sailed a small boat across the Mediterranean to North Africa. The boat sank before he reached the shore, and he swam the last few miles. Staggering onto an isolated beach, he managed to find a British patrol in an otherwise empty desert. The story was told with humility and some emotion.

He was a good storyteller, and it was a wonderful story. It reminded me of my early schooldays during the war. We were told in class that a boy who'd left school only a year before to join the army had escaped from Greece and rowed a boat across part of the Mediterranean, before being picked up. His name was David Humphreys. He was clearly a hero. We didn't know quite where Greece and the Mediterranean were, or what he was doing there, but the story stuck in my mind. And I remember my father telling me about families which had telegrams delivered to them, saying that a son had been killed or posted missing. That stuck in the mind too.

Anzac Day is a reminder of these events. Even if it's not always understood, it's a day which remains respected in a very different Australia. People sense that it commemorates some important and sad things. It's been described as Australia's secular Easter. Alan Seymour called his moving play about Anzac Day *The One Day of the Year* and, try as we might, it's hard to find a day which competes with it for solemnity and national soul searching. Australia Day doesn't. It should really be a day of celebration. On Anzac Day, which commemorates futility and sadness, returned servicemen and women march, under the colours of their wartime units, in the towns and cities of Australia. For them it's a reunion and a remembrance. As the years pass the ranks grow thinner, but the spectators, many of them children and grandchildren of diggers, still come. It's a moving occasion. They are there to show respect.

The day is partly about remembering overseas military service by Australian troops. They were always defending something or other, but there was frequent confusion about what that something was. At the end of the Great War, Billy Hughes thought it was to 'maintain those ideals which we have nailed to the very topmost of our flagpole—White Australia; and those other aspirations of this young democracy'. At the turn of the century more than 16,000 Australian volunteers took part in the Boer War, a disastrous war provoked by the British in pursuit of an empire in Africa. In Sydney, Cardinal

Moran wondered whether Australian troops should be 'expected to go to every place where a British war might happen to be carried on'. It seems that the answer was 'yes'. In the war of 1914–18, 330,000 Australians out of a total population of fewer than five million saw service in Europe and the Middle East. Sixty thousand died, 152,000 were wounded. Many of them were victims of incredible ineptitude by British politicians and generals.

The Anzac myth was born in Gallipoli, where 7000 Australians and 2500 New Zealanders died in a futile and misdirected military adventure. It's hard to see its relevance to the aspirations of a young democracy. The war in France was no less disastrous. The American historian Barbara Tuchman has captured its squalor, stupidity and horror. In *The Guns of August* she writes of 'the brutal, mud-filled, murderous insanity known as the Western Front'. For Australian troops it meant huge casualties, terrible conditions, and nothing gained. 'By then most of us thought that's it,' a digger on leave in England in 1918 recalled. 'We're not going back, we've had it.'

In 1991, I drove up on a sort of pilgrimage to Villers-Bretonneux near the Somme, to visit the Australian War Cemetery. It was a cold, bleak day. The land looked poor: the surrounding countryside had all the frosty charm of a moonscape. I walked in the drizzly rain up the slope amongst all those graves, half sad, half angry, trying to make a smattering of sense out of it all. In the village we were told that Australians were well remembered. They had come all that way to help save them from the Germans. A memorial service is still held there on Anzac Day.

In the early days of the war of 1939, the finger of the British Empire beckoned again. 'Great Britain has declared war,' said Prime Minister Menzies, 'and, as a result, Australia is also at war.' Australian troops fought in the Middle East, Greece and Cyprus. Thousands were taken prisoner in botched military operations. Our airmen fought with the Royal Air Force in the Battle of Britain and the bombing of occupied Europe. In the siege of Tobruk, under an Australian general, diggers recaptured some of the heroic flavour of Gallipoli. After Japan entered the war in 1941, Australia itself was in danger. Prime Minister Curtin recalled the troops from the Middle East to the Pacific. His announcement that 'Australia looks to America' was denounced as disloyal. But, for the first time and for the remainder of the war, Australian servicemen and women fought in the defence of Australia. The United States became our new military ally.

Later, Australian military contingents took part in wars in Malaya and Borneo in support of British colonialism; in Korea and Vietnam under American command; and, in January 1991, in the Gulf War. Korea, Vietnam, and the Gulf War were political offerings to the Americans. The Vietnam involvement was supported with spurious rhetoric about communist expansion and the threat to Australia. It was an American mistake for which 500 Australian troops paid with their lives.

The idea of Anzac Day developed quickly after the tragic failure of Gallipoli. The first ceremony was held a year later. Subsequently it embraced in its commemoration all those who served overseas, and especially those who died, in all those wars. The original Anzacs were swept up in the rhetoric of the British Empire. They were 'Soldiers of the King'. In the words of the World War I song, if the Empire called, 'Australia will be there'. In later wars the day had something to do with the American alliance. It changed from 'British to the boot heels' to 'All the way with LBJ'.

From the beginning Anzac Day was captured by the mythmakers of the Returned Servicemen's League. They gave the day its form and shape, and dictated its substance. The leadership of the RSL was predominantly drawn from the ranks of officers. There have been few representatives of ordinary ranks prominent in the organisation's eighty-year history. So the leadership assumed a right-wing posture on nearly every domestic political issue. Inquiries and criticisms about the possible shortcomings of World War I leaders were dismissed. The

RSL successfully lobbied in 1929 for the banning of the book *All Quiet on the Western Front*, a novel, narrated by a German schoolboy turned soldier, which portrays war as horrific rather than heroic. Later there were attempts to ban any books which 'defamed the soldiers of the empire'. Books about World War I were to be censored. In Australia's subsequent political skirmishes about the empire, the royal family, the anthem, the flag, the commonwealth and the republic, the RSL leadership has always been clattering the symbols of a confused conservatism. But, as time passes, and the generals and the colonels depart, the influences have grown weaker. Anzac Day is changing, perhaps remembering better things.

Australia and New Zealand have made more of the glories of overseas military expeditions than other countries. For fifty or sixty years Anzac Day was spoken of enthusiastically as a remembrance of the day Australia became a nation in the mateship and sacrifice of Gallipoli. But times changed. The composition of the Australian population changed. There has been a loosening of traditional bonds with the United Kingdom. The Vietnam War produced a thoughtful consideration of politically inspired overseas service. Australia has become more involved with its Asian neighbours, asserting a more independent stance. Historians began to question motives and critically examine the rhetoric about the forging of our national identity. Now those years seem wasted, the years of trying to make the Gallipoli tragedy a birthplace of nationhood. A veteran of Gallipoli and France, 100 years old in 1996 and very much alive and well, put it in these words: 'I suppose it's difficult to understand these days why young fellows would want to rush off to a war on the other side of the world. But at the time we saw it as a great adventure, as a chance to travel. We didn't think too much about the consequences of war.' He added, as an afterthought, 'There will always be aggressive people, I suppose, people who want power over other people.'

There's a powerful case for respecting others' great adventures, and it's admirable to be fascinated by the thousands of

Australian servicemen and women, plucked from ordinary occupations and pursuits, who served on the other side of the world. Their stories are recorded in books, diaries and radio programs, and in the archives of the Australian War Memorial. They are the real stories of mateship, sacrifice and egalitarianism. The sad part is the knowledge that so many died so young in pursuit of dubious causes. Young death is the saddest thing of human experience.

In 1988 I received a letter from Bruce Ruxton, president of the Victorian RSL, seeking my support for some not unworthy cause. I wrote back and said I couldn't help. I drew his attention to the RSL motto: 'The Price of Liberty is Eternal Vigilance'. I said I agreed with this and added, 'That's why I'm watching you.' We've been on friendly terms ever since. He has a sense of humour. It's just my sadness about Anzac Day is different from his. I find it sad that conservative spin doctors have used it for so long as a means, not just of remembering the past, but of rewriting it—and avoiding the future.

Never Mind, You'll Win Next Year

Grand Final morning. Spring is a few weeks old. From hundreds of Melbourne homes people stroll into the backyard and gaze anxiously at the sky. It might rain or it might not; it could be windy or it could be calm. Theories abound. Everyone's a bit of an expert. They're preparing alibis, hedging bets, laying the foundations for future arguments. It's been going on since the game began. *Plus ça change* . . .

I can't exactly remember the year I first attended a Grand Final. Not that it matters much. Not long out of school and a country boy, I was keen to witness one of Melbourne's great occasions. It was before television. I'd be able to describe the game to friends who were unable to be there—to be a bit of an expert myself. I bought a standing-room ticket in the old Southern Stand. I found myself on the concourse behind the seating area, and behind a lot of others with standing-room tickets. Nobody told me that standing room was not meant for short people. I had a splendid view of the backs of lots of heads, all bunched together like a crowd in a Tandberg cartoon. Mostly they looked like boofheads. Occasionally some kindly player kicked a towering punt and I had a glimpse of the ball. At the end of half-time, when the bars and toilets were still crowded with giant patrons, I saw the teams run back onto the field. That's about all. By the end of the day I felt discriminated against; I reckoned I'd been ripped off. I had nothing to tell my friends. I left the ground hoping none of them would ask me any questions about the game.

Nonetheless the day provided some compensations. The excitement and dismay of the partisan crowd gave me clues to the progress of the game. Supporters of the losing team increasingly invoked the help of some mysterious deity called 'Fokanel'. They kept calling out his name. The winning side seemed to be doing it on its own. I admired the way in which, with little spillage and no theft, glasses of beer were passed at shoulder level to thirsty spectators in the front rows. I consoled the inner man with a beer and hotdogs—not the plastic injection-moulded confections of today, but real snaggers, swimming like surfers in a drum of boiling water, rescued with tongs and stuffed into a crisp bread roll. But the decline of the hotdog is another story, mirroring the diffusion of football loyalties.

In the seventies, when sufficient old sports had passed on to make room for me in the Melbourne Cricket Club, I watched a Grand Final from the members' stand. Behind me two Melbourne supporters in their uniform of cavalry twill, reefer jackets, check shirts and striped ties were discussing politics, a different sort of game. 'I understand Leigh Matthews has joined the party.'

'That surprises me,' said his colleague. 'He looks a rough type. I assumed he was Labor.'

Later on, in the 1980s, being older, no taller and temporarily in good stead, I watched the game from a corporate box—

behind glass, noiseless, sanitised, crowd-proof with a business-class seat and a cinemascope view. There were Waldorf salads, chardonnay, trays of meat and of prawns, all cold, no hotdogs, not much passion.

From behind the glass curtain I tried to savour the slow build-up of tension in the crowd as the hands of the clock moved inexorably towards 2.30 p.m. It lacked the simple focus of the fifties. Instead the hallowed ground resembled a giant discotheque catering for every interest and emotion: the big screen for old and instant replays, marching girls, sky divers, banners and coloured balloons.

From the box, looking sideways, you could see but not hear the commentators in the broadcast booths. Legendary figures mimed a million words, told anecdotes a hundred years old, made predictions (Lou Richards doing for football what Malcolm Mackerras does for politics), and quarrelled over technical points.

Downstairs in the players' rooms, deep in the bowels of the stand, the atmosphere would be charged with the smell of liniment. Different tensions would be present in hearts and minds and hamstrings. Two coaches would be pacing the floor, pleading, flattering, cajoling, putting the final touches on a performance they and their audience knew by heart. Then the final slap up, some shouted words of encouragement, and the players would run down into the race, with trainers yapping at their heels.

The national anthem ends the foreplay and starts the game. The players line up in two opposing rows and fidget to the music. Supporters clear their throats for the first mighty roar. The commentators fall temporarily silent. Everyone is ready to contribute to the real spectacle about to take place.

The game starts and instant experts begin to pontificate on early trends. If the full forward fires, if the ruckman is reading the game well, if someone is seen to be carrying an injury—the speculation swings back and forth. The first goal is kicked and, in the words of an American observer, the man in the white fedora and laboratory coat steps forward and makes like Batman. The crowd begins to settle down, slowly dividing into the categories of the passionately committed, fixed on the outcome, and the agnostics, contemplating the process.

The passionately committed are the supporters of the two teams in the final. They have a stressful day. The agnostics are there for the finer points, to see a good game of football, and because it's a great occasion. They may take sides, but in a lukewarm sort of way. Sometimes they're already thinking of next year or the year after. Some day it may be their turn.

Hawthorn was the powerhouse of football in the 1980s and early nineties. My team, Geelong, bumped up against them in the 1989 Grand Final and lost by a narrow margin. It was worse than that. For Geelong supporters Hawthorn seemed invincible. They beat us again and again in home games and in close finals. They were professional, cool and unforgiving. Geelong, a talented side, seemed a victim of the Peter principle.

In 1992, the interloping West Coast Eagles became the new powerhouse, beating Geelong in the Grand Final of that year, and again in 1994. They played tough, skilled, precise football, rather like cybernauts. They reminded me of the medieval Italian artist Andrea del Sarto. He was known as 'the faultless painter', so predictably clever he became a bore. There's nothing boring or predictable about Geelong's football. But they do have a boring tendency not to win Grand Finals. Being a Geelong supporter is character-building. It heightens the capacity for suffering. But there is always hope. In a cupboard at home I have a demijohn of Cabernet Sauvignon grown at Bannockburn, near Geelong. I'm going to drink it when Geelong wins a Grand Final. It's top quality and they say it improves with age. The problem is I don't.

Grand Final night is for the winning team and its supporters. I've never celebrated a Geelong Grand Final win in the pub. Sometimes I've watched others enjoying themselves, with a tinge of envy, but also enjoying the occasion myself. After the

Essendon-Carlton final in 1993, for example, it seemed perfectly normal. That night I sensed that staying home might seem miserable, and slightly churlish. After all, it was the end of a wonderful week. It was a sort of watershed night. Sydney had just been awarded the 2000 Olympics and people felt good about that, about the spring weather and the Grand Final. Even the economic indicators seemed to look a little better. It was as if after years of stormy weather the dark clouds had rolled back revealing a patch of blue sky. The 1993 Grand Final was not a nail-biter. But there was some wonderful football. And the entertainment before the game and at half-time was professional, and—as it ought to be—entertaining. The Australian Football League seemed to have got it right. People were pleasantly surprised. The game itself was a triumph for youthful players. And it marked the end of a wonderful season for Aboriginal footballers, displaying unique talents like their musicians, painters, and track-and-field athletes. I liked the idea that a lot of people felt good about that too.

So we went to the local pub, which is not too far from the MCG. Inside it was packed. They spread across the road to the front of the laundromat and the Vietnamese general store. Everyone seemed extraordinarily happy. Well, almost everyone. There was a sad man sitting on a stool in one corner of the bar. He had a face and curly hair like Harpo Marx. His pale blue eyes blinked away at a fixed spot on the far wall, like a person trying to read an optometrist's chart. People were very solicitous about him. 'Leave him alone,' they said. 'He's probably a Carlton supporter.' Others thought he was a gambler who'd lost all his money. He was an object of curiosity and genuine concern. He seemed to make people slightly guilty about being happy. Some suspected he was very shrewd.

The best raconteur at the bar had been celebrating for a week. He'd played in the winning team in the Victorian Football Association Grand Final the week before. He'd kicked three goals and three points. The three points, he told us, were very important. The Grand Final had caught up with him, like a second wave, propelling him on to greater celebratory exploits. His stories, 'performed' with a deadpan face, were melodramatic and funny. He had a mate called Toss who bought him drinks while he recounted his achievements. Toss provided a sort of chorus function at the climax of each story. It was well done. A week's practice makes perfect. Others talked about going to the 2000 Sydney Olympics, as if they were about to happen next month. 'I'll be heading up there,' a youthful drinker told me. He was already planning his trip. Another more artful man, who was not looking so far ahead, asked me for an autograph for his wife. He insisted, as he put it, on 'dictating' it to me. He produced a pen and a tattered piece of paper and dictated the following: 'Dear Judy, I'm sorry you're not here tonight. It would have been nice to meet you. I've talked a lot to your husband and I have to say he's a terrific bloke. John Button.' Then he folded the paper carefully, and put it in his wallet, like a promissory note or a cheque to be cashed in at a later date: I guessed it would be the following morning. He went away with a happy smile on his face. Everyone except Harpo had happy smiles. They were contemplating the future: long, medium, and short term. Some were planning for next year's Grand Final.

All this gregarious stuff is part of the ritual, part of celebrating a great sporting occasion. Maybe Harpo thought it was all a bit superficial. Deep down he knew that it was the private emotions and private rituals of the true believers which really counted. Losing a Grand Final can be a terrible experience. People react in different ways. A Lebanese guy with a milk bar near the MCG told me he'd been standing outside his shop and seen a woman and a child about ten years old walking past immediately after the 1994 Grand Final. The woman had a Geelong scarf and a Geelong flag and the kid wore a Geelong beanie. As they walked past he noticed they were both crying. 'Never mind,' he said, 'you'll win next year.' He was a kindly man. He meant well, but it didn't work.

The woman turned around and glared at him. 'Why don't

you go and get stuffed,' she said.

My Lebanese friend was shocked. He'd heard the harsh voice of bitter experience. I understand how the woman felt. Next year is always too far away.

I don't know how I'd react to my team winning a Grand Final. I'd probably drink the bottle of red with a couple of mates: then go to hospital. I'd go to the casualty ward and ask to be admitted. I'd say I was suffering from shock. Losing I'm familiar with. I'm experienced. I leave the ground the moment the final siren sounds and slink quietly home. I sit in a chair staring at the wall. I go into deep recession. It's too painful to recall.

I even have a Grand Final ritual when my team is not participating. Again it's personal. A private experience.

When the game is over I leave the victors and the vanquished to wallow in their vulgar emotions, tuck my glossy Grand Final program under my arm and walk home. I put the glossy in a bottom drawer, and take out the *Football Record* for the last home-and-away match. It contains the entire statistics for the season just passed. For half an hour or so I contemplate the injustice of the world: if only so and so hadn't been injured in the first game, if only, if only . . .

Then I take a clean sheet of paper, draw a splendid oval, and write in the names of the best possible Geelong team for the following year. I discount the chance of injuries or suspensions, write in a couple of mythical recruits, and totally satisfy myself that the Cats will be in the finals next year. I know I'll go through the same routine again in the future because I've been doing it for a long time: it's becoming a habit. Then I slowly confront the growing horror of nothing to look forward to.

I'm Afraid, Love, That Horse Came Last

I imagine I looked slightly furtive and a bit confused when I walked out of the local TAB that November afternoon. It was a long time since I'd been in a TAB. This one was crowded with Vietnamese and a few old ocker diehards. They all seemed to know precisely what they were doing. I had no idea. The place resembled a packed video parlour. A TV screen blared in the corner. There were monitors all round the walls, showing fields and results in Melbourne, Randwick, Doomben, Adelaide and Ballarat. It all looked so complex that I felt you'd need to do a two-year diploma to understand it properly.

I knew, however, what I wanted to do. I wanted to put five dollars each way on a horse in race three at Flemington. A friend had given me a tip on an outsider. 'No more than two dollars each way,' he warned. I'd decided to lash out and make it five. It took me a while to find the right form, which I filled in with great care. I detected some impatience from the men in the queue behind me who were waiting to fill out their forms.

I took the form up to the woman at the counter. 'That race is over,' she said.

I looked around at the incomprehensible monitors. 'Could you possibly tell me which horse won?' I asked.

'Of course I can,' she said obligingly. She studied a screen. 'I'm afraid, love, that horse came last.'

I felt better. I had one more tip for race four. I filled in another form and took it to the counter. It seemed a big transaction: like buying your first jellybeans at a sweet shop. I felt that the woman behind the counter understood. She was very kind.

I went home and watched the race on TV. My horse was very consistent and ran second last all the way. I turned off the TV. 'That's the end of the season for me,' I muttered sadly to myself. It had been a short season. It had only begun ten days before at the Melbourne Cup.

I'd not been to a Melbourne Cup before. In fact I'd never been to the races except for a couple of country meetings, and on one afternoon in Bangkok. I'm not sure why I went in Bangkok, but I suppose I was at a loose end. I found it very bewildering. As far as I could see I was the only non-Asian racegoer.

Fortunately, a man sitting next to me spoke English. He produced the race book and went through the field in each race and marked particular horses, which all had the same owner. 'He's the chief of police,' he said. 'They're the only horses worth backing. If he has more than three horses in any race, don't bet.'

I observed that the chief of police owned a lot of horses. 'Doesn't the racing authority impose some limitations?'

'He runs the racing authority,' said my new-found friend.

Perhaps this is why I've shied away from racing and found it so difficult to understand. I've always felt you needed inside knowledge.

At Flemington on Cup Day I strolled around to get my bearings. It was very wet. I waded through a lake across to the track, watched some horses being exercised, walked round the horse stalls, and made an early reconnaissance of the betting ring.

My reconnaissance revealed amazing scenes. The dress was very fancy. And there's something quite incongruous about people in their best clothes standing in puddles and tippy-toeing through the mud and slush. But Australians handle adversity better than success. One well-dressed lady had embarked on a hair-raising adventure. She'd tried to protect her outfit from the wet by clambering along a cyclone wire fence at the edge of a huge puddle. Halfway across the puddle she got stuck. She looked like a prisoner of war in drag trying to get out of Stalag 17. Any moment I expected a shout. 'Pig dog Englander, vat are you doink?' But there were no shouts, no guards: just two gentlemen untangling her. They were in morning dress and up to their ankles in water.

I visited several marquees where people were having lunch. They were mostly eating prawns and pressed chicken. There seemed to be an abundance of excellent wine, which was generously shared around. Everybody gave the impression of enjoying themselves.

In the betting ring I sized up a few bookies before choosing one with a short reliable-sounding Anglo-Saxon name. My wife approached the bookmaker first, hesitating as she made up her mind for the last time.

'Better tell the lady what to do,' said the bookie.

'I know nothing about it myself,' I replied.

'That's the best way to be, mate,' he said.

I put a bet on a horse called Air Seattle. The bookie grinned and said, 'You'll be back later with this ticket.' I gave him a knowing wink. For a moment I felt like an insider. Then he caught the eye of someone standing behind me. 'Jack Murphy, four hundred each way on number 12,' he shouted. I turned around. The man I took to be Jack Murphy was nattily dressed. He had a floppy red hanky in his top pocket, a red bowtie and a matching red face. He looked in the know. I raced up to another bookie and put a fiver on number 12.

In the crowd I got talking to a friendly man who said he was the owner of a horse called Frontier Boy. 'How do you think he'll go?' I asked.

He said the horse was being ridden by a jockey from Hong Kong who thought it would do well. 'We think it might get a place,' he told me. I put an each-way bet on Frontier Boy.

I watched the race from the Hill Stand. I had the interesting experience of all my senses failing at once. I couldn't see the numbers clearly. I couldn't hear the race caller above the babble of competing transistors, and I couldn't remember the horses I'd backed. As it turned out, it didn't matter.

I don't suppose I expected to win. But I went with all sorts of other preconceptions about the Melbourne Cup. I expected more formality, and lots of fenced-off areas which ordinary mortals couldn't enter. I imagined looking through a fence at a crowd of post-colonial toffs aping, in dress and demeanour, the English upper-classes. In fact it turned out to be one big, friendly and very Australian party. There were only two obvious classes: those who were drunk and those who were sober. In between, there was a large, lumpen middle-class at various points on the sobriety curve. I suspect they enjoyed themselves the most.

I was slightly shocked by people I met at Flemington who hadn't watched the races at all, even on television. They spent the day socialising in marquees. For them the day was a big excuse for a party. The miserable weather merely added to the challenge. A sociologist I know would probably have described it all as a big urban middle-class fantasy: all those tents and marquees, and flashy guys with banknotes, and people stumbling round in the mud like diggers on the goldfields. But it seemed so much better than the solitary mania of the pokie players. Fantasies which work have a lot going for them.

I left Flemington carrying an old canvas bag in which I usually carry my tennis gear. The thought crossed my mind that it probably looked like a bag full of money. It would be just my luck for someone else to think the same: some disgruntled amateur mugger. Then I realised that he wouldn't have any luck either. All the bag contained was a tattered plastic raincoat and a pair of old gumboots. I felt like a digger on the goldfields, unsuccessful, but nonetheless a digger. I had my gear, and a touch of the fever, and I thought I'd like to try it all again.

Christmas Wasn't Meant to be Like This

Busy people do their Christmas shopping late. That's my theory, based on observation and experience. The workaholic views an approaching Christmas Day as more like Armageddon than a festival. Things have to be done: the last phone call, a final letter, the desk to be tidied ready for a new year.

I don't have much excuse for this kind of behaviour any more. But old habits die hard. This year I decided it would be different. I devised a plan for my Christmas shopping. It would be high speed and low cost. At unwrapping time it would be egalitarian as well. All my friends and relatives would be given the same present. I thought about the magic, high-speed, low-cost, egalitarian present for some time before deciding on Kazuo Ishiguro's enchanting novel, *The Remains of the Day*. It would be good for them: enjoyable and uplifting. Uplifting in the sense that one's spirit is raised by a great artist . . . like Mozart, Van Gogh, Miles Davis, Ablett or Pavarotti.

I imagined the grateful smile on the face of the bookseller, when I asked, 'Have you got a novel called *The Remains of the Day*?'

'Yes,' he would say.

'OK. Then I'll have twenty copies, wrapped separately.' All done in one hit.

At 2 p.m. on Christmas Eve I went to my favourite bookshop. I asked for the book.

'Sorry,' the woman said, 'we're out of stock. You could try elsewhere.'

I tried another bookshop, and received the same answer. I raced from one bookshop to another without success. Thwarted by the perverse cunning of the book trade I paused to take stock over a cappuccino. Reluctantly I pulled the emergency list of Christmas requests out of my pocket.

It included various items of clothing, Lego for a favourite child, the book of a film about water and chocolate, perfume, CDs, more books, spirits for those inclined to conviviality. I divided these miscellaneous objects into groups, on the back of a cardboard drink coaster. I marked it 'List B'. I decided on perfume as a new generic present for female relatives and friends. I planned the order in which I would make my purchases. Returning to the favourite bookshop I asked for iced water and hot chocolate. The woman looked at me with a pained expression. I realised I'd given my usual order at Pellegrini's on a cold winter evening. 'Something like that,' I said.

'What you mean,' she said, 'is *Like Water for Chocolate*. I'm afraid we are sold out. You could try somewhere else.'

I began the rounds of the bookshops again. In each shop I received the same answer. In the end I settled for a book voucher. In a music shop I asked for a particular CD. 'We don't have that here,' the woman said. 'You could try somewhere else.' Finally, in another shop, I got what I wanted after pushing my way through a crowd of noisy teenagers jostling at the counter like Italians boarding a bus. At a chemist's targeted for my perfume purchases I was told, 'We don't carry that range.' I was directed to an expensive department store. There in the toiletries department I committed myself to the care of the young woman labelled 'Sandra', a psychotherapist masquerading as a shop assistant. 'How can I help?' she asked with a smile like a neck massage. This, I thought, is an understanding person. I pulled out the drink coaster. I began to explain. In fact, I began to blab. I told her the Christian names, the ages, temperaments, occupations, social preferences and demeanour of all the women on List B.

She smiled encouragingly. 'Which fragrance do you prefer yourself?' she asked, as she sprayed my hands, wrists and ears from various bottles.

'Nothing too special,' I said. 'Just good perfume.' She suggested alternatives—perhaps a small cake of fragrant soap priced at thirty-one dollars. I sensed it was time to establish what was left of my independence. 'Sandra,' I said pompously, 'you must understand that for a person of my age, Presbyterian upbringing, life experience and social attitudes it is quite impossible to pay thirty-one dollars for a cake of soap.'

She nodded understandingly. She put the soap away, and proceeded to sell me more expensive perfume. I left the shop in a fragrant and triumphal cloud.

All I needed now was the Lego. I tried two shops without success: 'Sold out.' In a third shop the man said, 'We've only one set left. It's rather expensive.' At 6 p.m. I staggered out of the shop with a suitcase full of Lego. The streets were suddenly empty. Shops were closing. The city seemed as if it had suffered a direct hit from a neutron bomb. It had hit my wallet as well.

I must say that all this took its toll. I'd walked for miles. It had been an action-packed afternoon. I'd suffered numerous indignities and frustrations. I felt tired and slightly emotional. I needed a drink. In fact I deserved one: just a small one to help the transition from the sordid world of commerce to the warmth and friendship of the Christmas spirit. I popped into the nearest pub. Later I met some friends for dinner at a restaurant. It was warm and friendly. I remember the laughter and too much food. I can't recall much else, except that someone described me as 'a congenital gentleman'. I remember that because, unaccustomed to exotic and gratuitous compliments, I wrote it down on a paper napkin. I found it in my pocket the next morning.

We'd been invited, after dinner, to a Christmas Eve party: a special party where we would drink eggnog in the North American tradition. A doctor friend, a law-abiding man of boulevard self-assurance, said he would drive. But only if his personal breathalyser device, which he kept in his car, showed a satisfactory reading. He blew in the apparatus three times. Each reading was different. They were all well below the limit. 'I can't believe it. The bloody thing must have a hole in it,' he announced with a professional air. We navigated our way very slowly through back streets to the party. The charming hostess poured me a glass of eggnog. It tasted rich and Christmassy: something between a zabaglione and a vanilla milkshake. I poured myself a second glass. These North Americans know how to do it, I thought. I poured myself a few more. I remember spooning a colourless liquid into my glass from the bottom of the bowl. Later a good samaritan called Stephanie drove me home.

On Christmas morning I felt queasy. I decided to forgo the pain of jogging. I didn't feel much like breakfast either. In church, an hour or so later, I began to develop symptoms of a serious illness—a thumping headache, possible brain damage, sickness in the stomach, aching limbs. 'Hark the Herald Angels Sing' brought on an attack of nausea. 'O Come All Ye Faithful' seemed to single me out from the rest of the 'joyful and triumphant' congregation. There was a story for the children. It promised jelly babies for children who were good over Christmas. I had problems in distinguishing the lessons from the sermon. One thing merged into another. I yearned for the mystery of the Latin Mass, equally incomprehensible to everyone. The priest prayed for the country, and for the government and the opposition. I leaned forward in a desperate attempt at concentration. He prayed for the new treasurer. 'Amen,' I burped in a reflex spasm of tribal loyalty. He prayed for the suffering people in Bosnia and Somalia, for the sick and injured in hospital, and for those for whom the day held out no hope. Any moment, I thought, he's going to mention me. I waited tactfully until the offering had been collected, then slipped out the back door during a hymn. I called on some friends for a quick glass of festive soda water before heading for home. In the car I reflected sadly on all those people at Christmas feasts, exchanging pleasantries across the generation gap. For lunch I ate a small banana, one of those sugary ones. Then I went to bed.

At 4 p.m. I got up and began parcelling my purchases ready for the next round. My hands shook as I grappled with unwrappable objects of grotesque shape. I used yards of sticky tape. My presents looked like patients in a casualty ward. I cursed the inadequacies of the book trade, which had aborted my master plan. I struggled to remember the names for the Christmas gift cards. Clearly what I needed was a hair of the dog. I pondered on the meaning of the expression. Did it just mean an alcoholic drink, or did it mean an actual hair of the actual offending dog? I decided it was better to play it safe, and looked up 'eggnog' in a recipe book. The list of the ingredients which began 'Take one raw egg' quickly convinced me that I'd made a mistake. But then, what was new about that this Christmas?

I poured myself a whisky. Slowly I began to feel better. In fact I felt deliciously numb. It induced a sense of philosophic calm. One thing's for sure, I thought, there will be no jelly babies for me this Christmas. Maybe it's all a learning experience: an eggnog experience.

On the kitchen table there was a card from a Jewish friend with a Santa Claus on the front. The Santa looked like Rappaport. 'Two thousand years ago,' Santa was saying, 'Christmas wasn't meant to be like this.' For the second time that day I said, 'Amen.'

Modern Life

Want It with Garnish?

Food glorious food
Hot sausage and mustard
When you're in the mood
Try eating some custard

NOTHING MUCH has changed. If Oliver Twist were alive today, and living in London, he'd be well advised to stick to hot sausage and mustard: or perhaps just mustard, which is an English specialty. And he'd have to be in a very good mood to try the custard. Sadly the British don't have a reputation for high-quality cuisine: in fact they've developed a reputation for the exact opposite.

Across the Channel in France cooking and eating are a central part of the culture. The French are very good at them. Food is a source of great national pride. I doubt if there are many other countries in the world which have the equivalent of a *chevalier du fromage*. France invented the idea of *cordon bleu* and boasts cellarmasters of international renown. Somehow there is always fresh bread, fresh fruit and fresh vegetables. I suspect it's the distribution system which puts these products into their competitive network of fascinating food markets on a daily basis. They start with fresh ingredients and they know how to cook them.

In Italy and Spain there are specialist national cuisines of distinction. Italy, like France, has made an export industry of food. In a word association game, say 'French' and people say 'frogs'; say 'Italian' and people say 'spaghetti'. No other countries in Europe enjoy quite the same international reputation. You have to go east to countries like India, China, Japan and Malaysia to find similar examples of distinct and renowned national gourmet cultures. If you keep going further east to the United States you find yourself in a country where the food culture is based on quantity rather than quality. Americans seem to eat too much too quickly. Their fast food culture is going well. McDonald's is a national icon. What's good for McDonald's is not necessarily good for America.

Australia seems to have escaped the Anglo-Saxon grease-trap. Sometimes we forget how lucky we are. The choice and quality of fresh food here is as good as anywhere else in the world. And it is cheap by international standards. It is carried through in the choice and quality of restaurants which, in turn, partly reflect the contribution of migrants from countries with strong food cultures, such as China, Italy, India, Vietnam and sometimes France. We're lucky that English and German migrants have involved themselves in businesses other than restaurants. They're better at other things.

Since the time of European settlement Australians have usually enjoyed an abundance of food: the early settlers found it tough going, waiting for supply ships, scratching round in arid soil, trying to create an English Garden of Eden in a harsh and unfamiliar environment. They muddled through on a simple fare, heavy on meat, potatoes and boiled vegetables. As the years passed things got better—but the variety, and to some extent the quality, of our fresh food is something of fairly recent origin. It belongs in the second half of the twentieth century, mostly to the last twenty years.

As a child, compulsorily at church, I would gaze on Harvest Festival Sundays at the table in front of the altar, laden with sheaves of wheat, pumpkins, large marrows and shiny new potatoes. It was a special occasion. The idea was that we should thank God for the abundance of the land, and the food which it produced: a local downmarket version of Thanksgiving in America. Uncooked, those vegies didn't look too appetising. And there was not a great choice. It was not an experience which made the mouth water. It took a while to understand that it was all symbolic. The reality came with the cooking.

On Sundays for lunch there would be a roast: lamb or beef, or chicken on special occasions. For dinner we'd have cold leftovers from the lunch. Each of those meats had something deliciously special which went with it: mint jelly with the lamb, Yorkshire pudding with the beef, and bread sauce with the chicken. And they all had roast potatoes, gravy and 'greens'.

If we complained about the quantity, my father would tell a much repeated Mark Twain story. 'Mark Twain,' he would say, 'came from a very big family. He once claimed he was twenty-one years of age before he knew that a chicken had any other part but the neck. You should be thankful there are only three of you.' We never complained about the quality. It was all good food. And very British. In a town in country Victoria we had the best of British cuisine. It's probably never been the same since.

In our wildest imaginations we could not have contemplated the variety of good food available in Australia today. Something called macaroni cheese was the nearest thing to Italian food. Curry, a yellowish liquid originating in a packet, was enough to turn you off the subcontinent for life. Rice pudding was the closest we got to Chinese cuisine. French toast, a breakfast treat on special occasions, gave no hint of the world of *cordon bleu* chefs.

Eating out was always special, but it wasn't much better. Cafes were the place to go. In nearly every country town in Australia there was a cafe called Victory, Liberty or Dominion. Sometimes there would be one called the Parthenon. They were all owned by Greek migrants. I used to think that Greece must be the biggest country in the world. So many surplus cafe proprietors. None of these cafes served Greek food. You had a choice of steak, or steak and eggs, or sausages, or steak and sausages, or sausages and eggs. Tomato sauce added a touch of colour and high-living. There was an optional extra called garnish, a handful of limp shredded lettuce.

'Want it with garnish?' the waiter would say. It was wise to say yes; important to eat your greens.

In the sixties the late Robin Boyd told me that he had taken a European visitor to a country hotel for lunch. Boyd asked the waiter for a bottle of claret. The waiter returned a few minutes later with the news, 'You're stiff mate, there's none in the fridge.' Australia now has a world-class wine industry of which Australians are justifiably proud. Its reputation has grown in the last fifteen years. There are some astute consumers. We produce a range of cheeses and dairy products which is second to none. We have a rich variety of sea foods. We enjoy the benefits of both tropical and temperate climates for growing food: bananas in Queensland, apples in Tasmania. Quicker and more efficient transport allows for distribution of fresh food across the country. The influence of migrants from various countries and the fact that Australians are compulsive travellers have helped create a demanding market for high quality and distinctively prepared food. Australia, which used to confine itself to being a producer of commodity foodstuffs for export, and plain Anglo-Saxon fare for the home market, now produces an extraordinary array of different products. And Australians spend about $33 billion a year on locally grown food: everything from pistachio nuts to pecorino cheese, Atlantic salmon to alpine strawberries, olive oil to organic fruits, emu to eggplant. Australia probably produces as wide and exotic a range of food as any country in the world.

As Robert Hughes, the historian and critic has pointed out, 'nobody ever went to Australia to enjoy its cuisine'. In the last decade or so 'visitors have been pleasantly surprised, even enraptured, by it'. Mostly the transformation is a consequence of immigration which has created new and diverse demands for food, but also brought the capacity and skills to grow it. Fine food growing is based on small enterprises, like backyards, market gardens, orchards, the little stainless steel factories of boutique cheese-makers. Together with better and more adventurous chefs, all this has changed Australia from a 'culinary monoculture' to a 'mosaic'.

There are still, of course, some mind-boggling realities of consumption of mass produced meals. At a Melbourne football final the crowd consumes seven kilometres of hotdog sausages, tonnes of bread and a bathtub full of tomato sauce. Airlines still serve salads which are weary, flat and unpalatable. There are plenty of institutional meals which taste like they've been cooked in Alice Springs and piped around the country like invoices once were in the pneumatic tubes of shops. Perhaps this is inevitable. But good choices are available. And there's an opportunity to establish Australia's reputation as a country with a strong and different food culture.

Abundance and choice are a secular and contemporary manifestation of the symbolism of Harvest Festival Sundays half a century ago. We should be thankful and enjoy them. Growing diverse and interesting food, cooking, eating and drinking are each long-cultivated human arts. Eating is part of civilised leisure. Victims of the global neurosis can probably get by without much civilised leisure. These days the shelves of pharmacies are marvels to behold. Health care tablets can fix almost anything—cramps, eyes, cold sores, backache, acidity, kidney and bladder, hair, insomnia, anxiety, constipation, colds and flu, menstrual pains, sinus and body building. There's a tablet for every one of them. A careful selection will probably keep you alive, save time and ensure a joyless life.

Australians are increasingly preoccupied by the prospect of an electronic future, and what it means in terms of jobs, work organisation, entertainment, and distribution systems. They're issues appropriately considered over a good meal. If it all gets too depressing a bottle of wine will help, and lead perhaps to philosophic musing about how, in a changing world, it's important to hang on to the good things we have going for us. The food industry is one of these things. But we shouldn't be complacent about it. The enemies of quality are always at the gate.

What the Surgeon-General Said

I was waiting for a woman to finish her phone conversation. I couldn't help overhearing. 'Bruce,' she was saying, 'you've just got to stop eating red meat.' I pricked up my ears. 'I'm quite convinced that meat is causing your sinus problem.' There was a short silence. I guessed that Bruce was not convinced. 'Well, if you must know,' she said, 'an Indian woman told me. They know a lot about these things. For once in your life take my advice.' She hung up and glared at me triumphantly. She'd been managing Bruce's risks for him. She felt good about it. His life would be more comfortable. Perhaps he would live longer. I could imagine her saying 'I told you so' in a few years' time.

More and more people seem to give advice about the management of life's risks. If they feel their advice is insufficiently authoritative they're likely to cite an overseas source: an Indian woman, an ancient Chinese or an American. It doesn't seem to help all that much. The average life expectancy of Australians has in fact declined slightly in the last thirty years. Perhaps we're worrying about all the advice we get. It's no longer permissible to live to ninety-three by doing what comes naturally.

In China and most of Asia life expectancy is increasing. In Africa it is probably declining. In half the world it could be improved by eating more; in the other half by eating less, or differently. Forty thousand people die every day from starvation and associated diseases. Because the nexus is more difficult to establish, there are no figures for the total number who die from illness associated with over-consumption. A technocrat might describe it as a distribution problem. In a sense it is. It's also a moral problem. And it's going to get worse; the world's population is expected to grow by three billion people over the next thirty years.

In developed countries like Australia we know more about the tragedies in the underdeveloped world than we used to. Television makes sure of that. But the TV images don't necessarily help us understand. Perhaps because we don't have much real experience of starvation. We can switch off or change channels to a program closer to our own experience. We've learnt to live with road-accident statistics, deaths from heart attacks, and common diseases of the developed world. It's the dramatic and exotic illnesses which excite the most anxious attention. A while ago, for example, the media were full of news about a disease which seemed to eat people. Six cases of the disease, a deadly 'flesh-eating' bacteria, were reported at Colchester in England. It sounded horrible. We looked at the next day's bulletins to see if it was a plague which might be coming here. Experts were consulted. Reassuring professors of medicine appeared on television. They said it was a rare disease which had been round for a long time. It could be treated if diagnosed early on. 'Not to worry,' they seemed to say.

Focusing on the smaller realities which seem more likely to impact on our own lives is not as easy as it might seem. There's too much confusing advice. Years ago, for example, I gave up eating butter, and transferred to margarine. I denied myself the simple pleasure of bread and butter, compensating with the medically induced virtuous feeling that margarine is better for you. My doctor friend, the one with the personal breathalyser in his car, used to nod at me approvingly. Then I read in a recent American magazine article that margarine is loaded with 'trans fatty acids'. The name itself sounded menacing. I read on and discovered that trans fatty acids have homicidal tendencies. They can kill people. The article left, as it were, a nasty taste in the mouth. I felt bitter and misled. So I've worked out a compromise. I've given up reading American magazines. I've started eating butter again, and margarine from time to time. It may be reckless and foolhardy. But the article could be wrong. It's all part of a balanced risk management strategy.

Recent pronouncements from Australian medical researchers persuaded me that a glass or two of wine a day is good for you. It seemed a civilised and palatable conclusion. I commenced a new drinking regime in a San Francisco restaurant with a bottle of Californian wine. It certainly induced a sense of well-being. The waiter left the empty bottle on the table, and I noticed the label flashing in the candlelight like a traffic sign. 'Government warning,' it flashed at me. 'The Surgeon-General says . . . ' The Surgeon-General said a number of things. In particular he said that drinking may be a health hazard. Now I've given up American wine in favour of the local life-enhancing elixir. I'm convinced that Australian doctors are more in touch than the Surgeon-General. I think he might be getting on in years.

Of course, Americans see things differently. The *New York Times* said that American experts think the deadly flesh-eating bacteria is 'making a comeback in the United States'. Drinking and smoking are much publicised risks there. Overeating and shooting people seem more acceptable in America than elsewhere in the developed world. In the United States the death risk from asbestos is said to be less than being hit by a falling aircraft. The risk from many of the toxic substances identified by the United States Environmental Protection Agency is 'no greater than . . . from drinking a cup of coffee'. It all makes sense. If you've drunk American coffee you know exactly what they mean.

It's hard to know what to do about all of this. The most way-out solution is to stop eating or drinking altogether. Then we'd understand the trauma of starvation better, and scamper back to our dangerous diets of plenty of food, wine, beer, coffee and the rest. That way we'd have something to worry about. My friend, who overdosed on vitamin tablets, says he's now concentrating on his 'calorie deficit'. I think he finds it hard work, which is probably good for him. The man who comprehended total risk management in Australia better than anyone was Norm from the 'Life Be In It' campaign. He seemed to approach it all with philosophic calm. I hear a rumour that he might be coming back and I hope it's true. He seemed to me to be a great Australian.

The Last Australian Smoker

In Australia we don't seem to have a Surgeon-General. Instead the 'government' is identified as the guardian of health and purity. On aeroplanes it is a government directive which bans smoking. There are government warnings on cigarette packets: 'Smoking Kills', 'Smoking is Addictive', 'Smoking Causes Cancer'. What would a government know about it? A Surgeon-General sounds more authoritative. But the government gets the money from tobacco excise. Maybe it's entitled to advertise as well.

Not long ago I was browsing in one of Sydney's few surviving quality bookshops. I picked up a paperback volume of short stories and opened it at the first page. The story, by the American writer Garrison Keillor, began, 'The last cigarette smokers in America were located . . . in the High Sierra by two federal tobacco agents in a helicopter who spotted the little smoke puffs just before noon.' Chilling stuff. And Keillor is supposed to be a funny writer. I read on, until the gaze of a severe shop assistant forced me to buy the book. The helicopter radioed a ground team. Six members of a crack anti-smoking joggers unit surrounded the smokers in their hide-out. They were tear-gassed, arrested and subjected to abuse and other indignities by a para-fascist tobacco agent. 'What does it take to make you understand?' he demanded. The warnings had been on the packets for years.

'That's America for you,' people might say. Anything can happen in America, where they take things to excess. It couldn't happen here. Australians are more tolerant. And yet, if you notice those dejected little groups standing outside 'smoke-free' public buildings, having a cigarette and catching pneumonia, it conjures up images of Orwell's *1984.* In Parliament House, Canberra, the female librarians and staffers smoked under the arches of an outside courtyard, one or two under each arch. I used to tell them they looked like hookers. I christened the courtyard 'Montparnasse'. I liked the idea. It gave the place a charm which it otherwise lacked.

As you get older and have less future to think about, you tend to think more about the past. Sometimes, for example, I wonder where all the Stalinists have gone. They can't all be dead and buried, or working as stockbrokers in the city. There are obviously a few surviving in places like North Korea, the former Soviet Union, perhaps China. But there used to be millions of them all over the world. And plenty in Australia. It would seem wrong if all those skills had been allowed to go to waste: adherence to a vision, however tarnished; the energy to pursue a myriad of mundane tasks for the cause; the talent for infiltrating and subverting other organisations; even justifying the odd purge of less enthusiastic colleagues. I tried to put myself in their shoes, to think about the moment when they lost the faith but kept some of the talents. Thinking about it like this, I worked out what had happened. They all went underground for a few years. Then slowly they came back into business as the anti-smoking movement: a classic popular front. Their self-appointed leaders have infiltrated the public service and federal parliament. They're going to create a better world. Lower echelons of the movement rattle campaign tins aggressively at traffic lights, put stickers on car windows and distribute leaflets designed to incite mass anxiety. It's the same old story over again. The means become more important than the end, the process more exciting than the outcome. But the new vision is no longer tarnished. It is, in fact, a smoke-free zone.

Smoking produces bad behaviour. At a whiff of smoke people glare at each other across rooms, indulge in moral posturing and flap their arms like goal umpires. In the Senate a few years ago I listened to speakers on both sides making excited speeches in furious agreement as they passed a regulation outlawing smoking in particular buildings. It sounded like they'd all been touched up by the invisible hand, and had, for the first time, a glimpse of the Australian Dream. Anti-smoking, it seemed, would unite Australia, provide us with a sense of national direction, re-create a moral purpose for the country.

I'm not in favour of smoking. I think it should be discouraged as much as possible. I think it shouldn't happen in confined and crowded spaces. I think smokers should ask other people if they mind them smoking. There are some new social norms which smokers should follow. But, in turn, I don't think they should have to put up with the moralising zealotry of retired Stalinists. Smoking goes back to the fifteenth century. Smoking inspired painters from Rembrandt to Cézanne. And probably since. Millions of people have derived pleasure from it. And, no doubt, millions have died from smoking, earlier than they might have. As they have from wars, sex, over-eating, and motor accidents. An Australian of rare distinction told me recently that he'd given up smoking on medical advice. He beamed happily at me and said, 'I'm so glad I smoked. It gave me great enjoyment over many years.' He seemed to me like a rational convert.

On a South African Airlines flight approaching Perth, I listened carefully as the purser announced that the cabin would be sprayed because of Australian quarantine regulations. Later he told the passengers to put any fruit in their possession in the bins on the concourse. And then he said, 'Ladies and gentlemen, in case you think Australia hasn't got enough regulations,

I must tell you that smoking at Australian airports is absolutely forbidden. Officers of the Federal Airports Corporation are empowered to impose severe penalties . . . ' He seemed to be laughing. I thought, this Afrikaner guy is having a shot at us. And he was right. Airports are sad and miserable places for Australian smokers. There should be designated places where smokers can smoke, just as there are designated places where drinkers can drink.

There's a need to find a balance in the argument. Some people are trying. At dinner with friends a couple of years ago the host lit a cigarette. People started to talk about smoking. A woman sitting opposite me, a pleasant woman from a good page of the street directory, with an endearing capacity to be socially shocked, told a story. She began hesitantly, as if not quite sure she should mention an indelicate matter. 'I was at a dinner party,' she said. 'This man sitting next to me lit a cigarette. I said to him, "How many cigarettes do you smoke a day?" He looked at me and said, "About twenty, but why do you ask?" I didn't quite know what to say, so I said, "Frankly I find it rather unpleasant".'

She paused, looked around, took a deep breath. 'Do you know what he said to me?' We waited anxiously. 'He asked me how many bowls of All Bran I ate for breakfast. So, I said, "Why do you ask?" Well, he looked at me coolly and said, "It's just that you've been farting all night. Frankly, I find it rather unpleasant".'

I think the whole thing was a totally new and shocking experience for her. But deep down I think she liked the guy. There was a real possibility of reconciliation.

I don't remember what happened to all the smokers in Garrison Keillor's story. One of them, a woman, was taken to court. The judge sentenced her to write an essay on self-discipline. She and her husband, who'd dobbed her in to the authorities for smoking, walked out of the court and started to cross the road. He was run down by a bus. You could hardly call it a happy ending. But there's a moral in it.

I Ticked the Box Marked 'Psychosis'

There are plenty of other health hazards besides food and cigarettes and grog: manholes without covers, cars, muggers, duck shooters, medical practitioners, cellular phones, and combinations of these individual hazards. There is always someone willing to tell you that one of these things is harmful. There are constant pressures to have something wrong with you. Feeling OK is almost indecent, and probably high risk.

It seems to be the same all over the world. On a trip to China a couple of years ago I had to fill in a health declaration. It said, '1. Please mark the symptom, if any, now: fever, rash, cough, sore throat, bleeding, vomiting, diarrhoea, jaundice, lymph-gland swelling. 2. Please mark the disease you are suffering: AIDS, Leprosy, Psychosis, Venereal Diseases, Active Pulmonary Tuberculosis.' You were clearly expected to have something. I read the form twice and became quite depressed.

I ticked the box marked 'Psychosis'. It seemed the most appropriate. I felt comfortable with it. The official on the desk looked at my declaration form, banged it with a rubber stamp, and gave me an idiotic grin. One happy soul to another.

Psychosis can, in fact, be a relatively benign disease and in its own way user-friendly. Lots of people have it and with practice you can regulate its intensity to suit yourself. Some people, however, just won't admit to it, as if it carried a stigma. Usually they develop a range of compensatory illnesses and disorders. I have a friend like that. He's extraordinarily rational and he would be mortally offended if you described him as psychotic. But he has a smorgasbord of complaints and special remedies and explanations. If he swims in the open he covers himself from head to toe to avoid the sun's rays. He wears a bathing cap. Once he turned bright pink during a board meeting. It had nothing to do with the sun. He said it was caused by an overdose of Vitamin B. He switched to multipurpose vitamins. He began taking a herbal antioxidant to combat the threat of unstable molecules in the body called 'free radicals'.

More recently he had a cold which he called bronchitis. It sent him on a downward spiral and he had to give up regular swimming. He grew fat without exercise and tried a short swim. He says he couldn't lift himself out of the shallow end of the pool and flopped back into the water like a common seal. When he went overseas recently he phoned me prior to his departure. He told me he was 'on' six tablets a day. His doctor said he had a 'wet chest'. He was worried about stopping over in Singapore with a wet chest. 'Never know what they'll do to you there.' I told him to be careful and ring when he got back. Now that he's back it's clear that he didn't take my advice. 'I swelled up in India. I just kept eating and drinking. You know how rude it is to say "no" in those countries. My chest has dried up, but I'm a living column of cholesterol.' It was not all bad, however. In Singapore on the way home a Chinese herbalist introduced him to ginseng. He's bought a reference book called *1800 Natural Remedies from Around the World*. He's very hopeful about the future. He anticipates a long and happy life. And he's not unmindful of others. He leaves strange but thoughtful messages on my answering machine:

> I'm just checking to see whether you've been to the gym today and whether or not you're building up muscle strength and particularly whether or not you're doing the squats because I'm very impressed with the latest work the gerontologists have done. And I think we should use you as a bit of an example of reversing the ageing process so we can prepare after all for the twenty-first century for you.

There's no doubt all this has become much more complex for people. When I was a kid psychosis and substitute disorders were less prevalent. Few people caught flash diseases like influenza, bronchitis and gastroenteritis. There were no viruses that we knew about. Usually you got a cold. It was either in the head or the chest. Sometimes it was in both. If a lot of people had a cold it was called a common cold. Nobody fell victim to the gastro. Whatever its form, it was called a bilious attack or, amongst intimates, 'tummy trouble'. There were other differences as well. You could sunbake without risk of skin cancer: the worst outcome was blisters and 'peeling'.

Whatever the illness the remedies were simple. If a cold in the head 'went to the chest' you were confined to bed. On the radio one would hear advertisements. A man with a hacking cough, for example, just audible above the sound of a howling wind, and then a voice over: 'When the wind howls down from the mountains, we of the Royal Canadian North West Mounted Police take a dose of Buckley's Canadiol Mixture'. The coughing faded. It sounded very macho and exciting. But it was a 'patent' medicine, not considered good for children. You stayed in bed without the benefit of patent medicines. If you suffered a bilious attack the cure was usually to 'block' or 'unblock' you, as the case required. Blocking was achieved with Kaomagna, which tasted like a mouthful of wet sand in a swirling surf. Unblocking was facilitated by 'salts' which tasted like a mouthful at Bondi on a bad day. Usually one got better quite quickly.

Simple remedies were underpinned by the prevailing ideology. In church the preacher gave straightforward warnings. 'It is easier for a camel to go through the eye of a needle, than for a rich man to enter the kingdom of God.' This we interpreted as meaning not to keep too much money in your money box. A life span was three score years and ten. Maximum. 'You know not the day nor the hour when the hand of the Lord will strike you.' This was confusing, but obviously correct: an eternal verity. As insurance you hung on to your mum's hand crossing the road. These days it seems an unfashionable philosophy, like communism or early Christianity. People try not to think about it. If you accept it then it's harder to swallow patent medicines, vitamin tablets, medical pontifications and warnings on packets and bottles. There doesn't seem to be much point.

Nowadays there's too much information, too much 'little knowledge'. You can watch diseases on the telly, or read about them in the weekend magazines. Illnesses are described in more complex terms. The cures are more complex too, with or without side effects. The medical profession obfuscates to maintain its mystique. Walking into a friend's office recently I found him trying to steam open an envelope over a cup of hot coffee. 'What on earth are you doing?' I asked.

He explained it was a referral note from one doctor to another. 'Just trying to find out what they're saying about me,' he said. 'Bastards never tell you anything.' I diagnosed his complaint as medically induced psychosis.

It's probably all gone too far: information overload is a terrible problem when it concerns your health. People turn towards herbal medicines, natural tonics, relaxation, the wisdom of the east. There is a need for a multi-purpose remedy. In Beijing a few years ago I thought I'd found one. It's called Long Er Wan. It says on the packet 'Royal Recite', which I think means 'Royal Recipe'—still, apparently, a good endorsement in China. When do you take the multi-purpose medication? It tells you on the packet:

> Effects and Indication: Invigorating the liver and benefiting kidney, strengthening the generative and preventing nocturnal emission, warming and invigorating the spleen and stomach, strengthening bones and muscles. It is suitable for impotence, weakening of sexual function, nocturnal emission, lumbago and pain of the knee, psychasthenia, insomnia, etc. (For details, see the explanation.)

I've never tried it. I'm keeping it, as it were, for a rainy day. A day, perhaps, when I have lumbago of the knee.

The Body Returns to Earth as Dust, You Fool

I don't have lumbago yet. I still go jogging which, of course, some people think is dangerous. There are plenty of warnings from non-joggers. Once, for example, I was in a car in Sydney. It was about six in the evening on that road which goes round the blunt end of Botany Bay. There were a lot of people jogging on the track beside the road. I said to the driver, 'There are a lot of joggers.'

'If you want my advice, Senator, I'd stay clear of that stuff,' he replied. 'I've got a brother-in-law who's an ambulance driver. Picks 'em up all the time. He's got a locker full of gym shoes.'

It often happens. You try and make polite conversation, and strike someone dedicated to catastrophe. I decided he was probably lazy, with the professional driver's dislike of any alternative form of transportation. Nonetheless, he'd made his point. It was six years ago and I remember it vividly.

Doctors are a bit the same. I have a seriously overweight cardiologist friend who sometimes gleams professionally at me from the rim of his beer glass and says, 'I'm not too sure about the jogging. Bit of a worry.' Orthopaedic surgeons are more convincing. They give you figures about the jarring of bones and joints: how many pounds per square inch of pressure is inflicted every time you put your foot down. But, of course, it all depends on how you do it, and where. And mostly they're talking about serious running.

My problem is that I'm committed. After all you have to do something. I don't play golf, or bowls, and weekend tennis gives way to watching football in the winter months. Swimming in a pool requires an infinite capacity for boredom. In Canberra I used to ride a bike, until two cataclysmic events changed my life. The first occurred one day when I was riding along in a happy trance, and a vicious territorial magpie struck me on the back of the head. Imagining I'd been shot, or hit by a flying saucer, I reacted by falling off the bike in a mangled heap on the roadway. Sadly, the incident took place right outside the Treasury building. As I picked myself up and examined my wounds, I looked up at the rows of Treasury windows. I imagined a hundred clerical assistants staring out at me and muttering, 'Serves him right. He was always sceptical about our forecasting. Never a true believer!' More importantly, it was Don Chipp's bike. Shortly after my unhappy accident, Don left politics and sold the bike. This upset me. I always felt I should have had first offer, but two messages in one month were enough. I gave up biking and reverted to jogging.

Jogging travels well. You can take it overseas with you. Sports like football and cricket don't travel to many countries. Golf does if you happen to be rich. Swimming is possible in certain places at certain times. But those six-metre hotel pools are too short even for me. And I've never been convinced that heavily chlorinated water with the consistency of warm saliva is actually healthy.

In Beijing, in the winter of 1988, I jogged one morning in the snow-covered grounds of the State Guest House. In the car, later in the day, the young Chinese protocol officer turned round from the front seat and said, 'Exchelenzy, when you are yogging you look werry young.'

I swelled up like a balloon. 'Thank you,' I said. This, I thought, is the wisdom of China. What a splendidly observant young man.

Then he added, as an afterthought, 'From the back.'

The balloon went down. Later I persuaded myself that it was better than nothing. Perhaps, I thought, in some other country, I'd encounter a young protocol officer with even finer diplomatic skills: one not given to second thoughts.

There's no better way to explore a foreign city than walking or jogging. If you're walking in normal clothes the locals think you're a tourist with a wallet full of money. Jogging in shorts and tee shirt suggests no money. And they probably think you're mad. They keep out of your way. And you see all sorts of interesting things. Jogging in Paris in the early morning I first understood the French passion for fresh bread. Nothing was open except the bakeries. I saw people scurrying home for breakfast with long loaves clutched possessively under their arms, looking like Don Quixote with his lance. In London the grass in the great parks is soft on the legs and ankles and there's always a monument to aim for across the park. In the streets you find the National Trust plaques on historic buildings. In Rome, the gardens of the Villa Borghese have grass and antiquities and up-market joggers in designer tracksuits. In Italy appearances count.

The word 'jogging' is often used loosely. It embraces a vast range of human activity. There are real runners who flash past you with a fanatical gleam in their eyes, serious joggers puffing along with a pained expression on their faces, power walkers obsessed with style, and cautious shufflers, swaddled in thick clothing, who look as if they'll never make it home before dark. And then there are the 'high tech' people, who jog with Walkman radios and look like zombies.

The nice thing is that you can make your own pace, adapt your own style, and as you get older you can kid yourself a bit. 'Where do you run?' people ask me in Melbourne.

'Round the tan,' I say with a flamboyant and imperial gesture, suggesting a quick marathon before breakfast. Afterwards I recall guiltily that I seldom go round the tan except at weekends. The rest of the week I take shortcuts through the Botanical Gardens. But there I can look at the plaques on the splendid old oaks, and the swans and ducks on the lakes, and feel good about Melbourne and the world.

I was once jogging in Central Park in New York. I stopped at a patch of grass and started to do some desultory push-ups. I was a little startled when a very large man emerged from the bushes nearby. He had a thick staff with a bundle tied in a red cloth at one end. He was dressed in an old and tattered greatcoat. His long hair and beard and bloodshot eyes gave him the appearance of Moses at the end of the long trek. To say the least, he was awesome. He stood there looking at me for a few seconds and then shouted, 'The body returns to earth as dust, you fool. Go home and read your Bible.'

'OK, OK,' I said, in that slow manner which Americans use when they mean, 'I hear what you're saying. I don't quite understand, and I'd like time to think about it.'

He stood glaring at me for a moment, then turned round and stomped off into the bushes. It was just as well. I was about to take off and become a real and serious runner with a fanatical gleam in my eyes.

The High-Tech Tenors

Polish pianists were said to be popular in the decade after World War I. Perhaps there was a Chopin-led recovery. T. S. Eliot wrote about it in his poem 'Portrait of a Lady':

> We have been, let us say, to hear the latest Pole
> transmit the Preludes, through his hair and finger-tips.

These fashionable pianists of the time played to discreet audiences in salons and small concert venues. The wider public had second-hand descriptions of their talents in newspaper reports, and social jottings masquerading as reviews. Occasionally they heard the music on scratchy gramophones. Actually seeing the artists was an elitist spectator sport.

In the 1990s there is a popular preference for Mediterranean tenors. Placido Domingo, Jose Carreras and Luciano Pavarotti sing to live audiences in Los Angeles, London or New York. Round the world their estimated television audience is about two billion people.

A few years ago, walking home through the streets of an inner Melbourne suburb, I had the feeling of being enveloped by the voice of Luciano Pavarotti. It was a hot night. Most of the terrace houses and cottages had their doors and windows open. Pavarotti was on television. The golden voice floated out into the narrow streets. Everybody in the neighbourhood seemed to be sharing the same experience, including me, who did but hear him passing by.

In a Los Angeles concert televised to the world, the three tenors displayed their masterly talents with a popular repertoire. They joked and sweated and teased each other—three confident stars at the top of their class. In the front rows of the audience one glimpsed the familiar faces of other stars of film and television: rich celebrities for whom being there was as important as the music.

Barry Humphries once described in a television interview how a responsive theatre audience ripples like a Mexican Wave. When people like an actor's jokes or a good line they turn their heads to the people sitting next to them. They like to make sure that their companions have enjoyed it too. Television viewers become similarly involved in a collective experience. They talk to each other about the songs, the artists and the audience. It's almost the same as being there. Thirty years ago the cognoscenti had a snooty disdain for what was then called 'mass entertainment'. That, of course, is what the three tenors were providing, through the medium of television. It is an enabling technology, allowing millions of viewers to see things which, for reasons of distance or lack of money, they might otherwise be denied. And it is almost egalitarian. In comfortable Australian suburban homes or in village halls in impoverished regions of the subcontinent, the chances are that people are watching the cricket or the three tenors at the same time.

Technology is not always enabling. It is not always egalitarian. Some people benefit from it. Others don't. There are old technologies which are good and new technologies which are bad. The rate of technological change in the last two decades has been so fast that it's hard to make informed choices. Sometimes we have a choice. At other times there is no choice available.

Common sense tells us, for example, that it's a good idea to wash your hands. Then you need to dry them. I've never had much success with automatic hot air hand-dryers. Often you have to queue up to use them. You wonder why the guy at the front of the queue is taking so long. When you get to use the machine you hold out your hands. It's a gesture of hope, when experience tells you it's not going to work. It doesn't. You end up drying your hands on a handkerchief or the seat of your pants.

Choice of technology is a pretty subjective issue. In public bathrooms the individual rarely has a choice. In homes, where people do have a choice, I've never seen an automatic hot air hand-dryer. As a piece of technology they've been around a long time. I remember kids talking about them, saying they gave you warts if you used them too much. On the positive side, they were said to circulate fewer germs than linen roller-towels. Germs were to be avoided at all costs. Disposable paper towels came later. They're quicker to use. More importantly, you feel in control of the process.

Australians are sometimes described as technological junkies. In the indulgent 1980s, many financial institutions and government departments invested vast sums in computer technology. Smiling representatives of multinational computer companies used to talk of 'the very sophisticated Australian market'. At the end of the decade some of the financial institutions went broke, suggesting that technology without wisdom is not sufficient.

In the 1990s Australia's rate of adoption of personal computers, faxes and mobile phones has been very high. We're big users of the Internet. Pay TV has been slower, which is perhaps good judgment. Much of this technology improves efficiency and productivity. It does things more quickly. People wonder whether it improves the quality of their lives. Technicians who understand particular new technologies marvel at the human ingenuity involved. Their eyes light up as they talk about it. The eyes of those who don't understand it glaze over. They absorb it slowly, if at all.

In the late 1970s the Australian government appointed a committee of inquiry into education, training and employment. The implication of the inquiry was that with the increasing pace of technological change the education and training system had something to contribute to community understanding. People had to be prepared for the impact on employment and lifestyles. The inquiry made some sensible recommendations. It thought that technology, properly handled, would create a whole set of new jobs. The report was mulled over for a while, and filed away. Some countries have technology assessment agencies. In Australia, a government body monitors developments in biotechnology. Otherwise it's left to the market place to decide. So theoretically you choose what you want. But for many people there's no choice. You get what you're given.

Last year the Australian Commission for the Future conducted research amongst young people. Technology change popped up as an important issue. It was seen as inevitable and alienating. It was something which would radically affect their lives, over which they had no control. The research material suggested a frightening absence of a sense of community, something to which people could belong. Technology provided no solutions. People spend a lot of time trying to find activities which provide a feeling of belonging to a community and of enjoying real experiences. The travel industry is a big beneficiary. But the anxieties of young people still blink away in the research reports like a warning lighthouse.

New technology has obliterated many occupations, deskilled others, and created a whole range of new jobs which are simpler, cleaner and quicker. New industries have emerged. But no developed country, with the possible exception of Japan, has handled the social impact very successfully. Economists say little about the impact of technology. It's difficult to measure dynamism with static models. They like the productivity gains, but find them hard to estimate. Counting the human costs is not their job. In Japan the models are different, resulting in sectors of their economy being notoriously inefficient. But in

Japan technology and economics are more subservient to social purposes.

The jargon of some technology buffs has a familiar ring. It hints at personal empowerment through adoption of something new. Empowerment is an idea used by purveyors of charismatic religions, feminists, academics selling short courses, and the gun lobby. Sometimes it works. A friend phones me every time he gets a new software package. It makes him feel good: 'more effective'. Then he rings up and says he's overweight.

The mobile phone is a good example. It helps people do business. Then you hear them ringing in the cinema, in restaurants, at the football. You see young men and women strutting up and down Macquarie Street or Collins Street talking frenetically into their phones. There's a whole new class of self-selected VIPs: people who are so important that they have to be constantly in touch. Their phone is a status symbol, the 1990s equivalent of an English gentleman's furled umbrella.

The three tenors represent 'broadcasting' in the best sense of the term: technology used for the best social purpose. But that may change. Recently I heard someone refer to the 'post-broadcasting era', which is soon to come upon us. I have a suspicion about what that means, but like many people I'm not quite sure. In my worst moments I think it means a period in which technology will give us such an abundance of so-called 'choices', tailored to individual preferences, that the habit of collectively sharing 'broadcast' experiences will begin to decline. On multi-channel TV there will be the technical capacity to cater for the private fantasies and whims of almost everybody. If you nurture a passion for fishing, star wars, home carpentry, pornography or basket-weaving, there will be a channel for you, ensuring that you become better informed and potentially more boring. We'll all be able to sharpen our minds by narrowing them.

The pokies, the personal computer, and the 'specialist' TV program essentially involve a one-to-one relationship with a machine. The regulars at the pokies have a strange, lonely and faraway gleam in their eyes. A personal computer is not called that for nothing. It has many uses, but socialisation isn't one of them. Mine bullies me, correcting my spelling, losing my letters, spitting out incomprehensible instructions like a Martian sergeant major, heightening a feeling of incompetence. With multi-channel TV you need a degree in specialist reading skills to comprehend the program guide, before locking yourself in to a private world. No-one else is involved in these experiences. These clever machines don't understand the human condition. They represent a further step away from the conventions of conversation and civilised social exchange.

J. D. Pringle in his book *Australian Accent* once described members of the professions in Australia, eminent in their particular calling, as unable to sustain an informed general conversation for more than five minutes. That was a long time ago, and he was describing the victims of a narrow vocational education system. The debate amongst educationalists about the relative merits of a general, as distinct from a vocational, education has been going on a long time. New technology potentially takes the debate a step further. It provides the possibility for everyone to be masterful in a narrowly focussed area of expertise. It limits the potential for conversation. 'What did you watch last night, my friend? The gardening program? I watched the program on advanced Esperanto.' If this is even half correct it doesn't make for a promising start. The so-called 'information rich' may become increasingly impoverished in social skills.

I suppose it's indulgent to reveal private nightmares which exaggerate the way the world goes. And perhaps it's not as bad as it seems. People can adapt to handling technology in a way which is comfortable for them. There's no longer a technological need to go to the cinema, but people still do because it's a shared social experience. Nobody has to lock themselves into their multimedia machine. You can always switch off. But, if no-one does, there will be an increasing danger of nothing to talk about.

New Paradigms in a Borderless World

The professor cleared his throat and looked over the top of his glasses at the businessmen and women assembled for the Saturday morning seminar. They were commerce graduates with several years' practical experience in their own businesses. The seminar was a refresher course, a good time to mention a few essential principles. He'd decided to remind them about the basic facts of the Australian economy, and give them some understanding of future directions. To keep it informal he told them they could interrupt with questions or comments. He thought it would be a good idea to deal with any anxieties they had at the beginning.

Many Australians, he began, are worried about the process of economic change. They are anxious about where it's all leading. This is because they lose sight of the goal of a completely level playing field. We must be unrelenting in pursuit of that goal. Business leaders should understand it even if others do not. He gave them a few facts and the reassuring observation that world trade would grow by 8 per cent a year in the next few years. This, he said, is good news. There's no reason why your business should not grow at the same rate.

One man seemed less than reassured. The professor remembered him vaguely from years gone by. He'd been one of his own students, always given to interrupting and asking questions. The only countries where this sort of growth has been achieved, the man said, are Japan, and the new economies of Asia, countries like Singapore and Malaysia. Didn't these countries all provide incentives and tax concessions to help develop nominated industries, to create employment and so on? Weren't they committed to long-term social and economic goals? This didn't sound like a level playing field. Would the speaker enlighten the seminar with some comments about these countries?

The professor cleared his throat again. A bit of frankness, he felt, would enhance his credibility. 'I know nothing about

Malaysia,' he said. 'I've never been there. There should, however, be no misunderstanding. The view of professional economists is that these countries have succeeded in spite of their policies.'

A woman in the front row giggled. Fortunately she'd not been one of his students. 'Where,' she asked, 'do all these professional economists live?' It seemed a stupid question, easy to answer.

'They live in Australia, of course,' the professor said. 'In fact,' he added, 'the view of professional economists is that the level of professionalism amongst economists in Japan and some of these other countries is extremely low.'

There were more giggles. 'Is there,' someone asked, 'an inverse relationship between the professionalism of economists and strong economic performance?'

'Well,' said the professor, 'it is difficult to generalise about these things. In big economies like the United States and Germany there is no such relationship. In fact in all the countries of the G7.'

'Who's in the G7?' another person asked. 'Isn't Japan a member?'

The professor couldn't quite recall exactly which countries were members. This was a memory slip. Something he'd have to check up on. Fortunately time had run out. The seminar adjourned for a coffee break. The professor packed up his overheads and left. The audience had not been quite as he'd expected. He'd go back to teaching students at his university. There he was a respected professor, indeed something of a guru.

I once heard some irreverent Internet fans refer to the occupation of lecturing academic as the 'sage on the stage', a role which might be rendered redundant by technology. It's a hardline position in which I don't quite believe. On the stage or the screen, academics will remain important. Like teachers, doctors, lawyers, and even some consultants, they have a certain guru status. They're paid to impart wisdom. But sometimes they know more about things which work in theory than things which work in practice.

It's the big international gurus operating on a world stage who fascinate me most. Just occasionally they're scientists, but mostly they're not. In one guise or another they've been around for a long time, mapping likely changes in the relationships between countries, guessing at new technological developments which will influence human life, picking long-term trends, winners and losers. Early gurus thought the earth was flat, a level playing field with a precipitous edge. Some espoused for a hundred years the phlogiston theory based on a non-existent substance which explained combustion—before oxygen was discovered. Others have speculated on the date when the world will come to an end. Some have founded cults and strange sects. The most enduring gurus have had a touch of humility. There are many examples.

The modern international gurus are increasing in number. They have lots of things in common with each other. Creatures of the global business economy, they spend a lot of time on aeroplanes, flitting from one potential client to another. Their suits are expensive but crumpled with travel, their pockets bulging with credit cards and airline schedules. They project models for every country or client based on their own background and education. Generally they use the United States as the most advanced model of human society, a 'benchmark' of economic and social progress. Some use European models. They charge a bit for their wisdom, and they drop names into seminars with a frequency which sometimes borders on carelessness. And they all speak English, a strange kind of English, which enhances the mystique of their presentation. From time to time I find myself listening to them, goggle-eyed with awe and anticipation. Perhaps I've listened too much. I am familiar with the parameters of what they have to say.

Mankind, a guru might begin, has to come to grips with a borderless world. Global business takes no account of artificial boundaries. I've discussed these issues with many business leaders. The chairman of XYZ, the fastest growing company in Central America, fully shares my views. I've discussed them with the president of Paraguay. Today I want to share my vision with you. Because the issues are difficult I propose to discuss them in an open architectural format. The need for a new socio-economic dynamic requires new initiatives of the will. The main threat to a new dynamic is zero-based thinking. Too many people look at the future with eyes of the past. This is a point I made recently to the finance minister of Nigeria. The 1980s have failed us: anticipations were not realised. The 1990s are slipping away. We are at a period of discontinuity. How do you lead people through a period of discontinuity?

Someone in the front row of the seminar shuffles in his seat, and decides to take advantage of the open architectural format. 'I understand precisely what you're saying,' he says, a necessary beginning when his company has paid $860 for him to hear the guru. 'But how do you explain this to ordinary people who don't understand global forces?'

The guru pauses dramatically, slipping an overhead back into its folder. He gives an encouraging smile to the questioner. This is, he says, just the point he was about to move onto. What is required is the development of a new paradigm. We need a new paradigm because people are not treated as valuably as they were. This is because the eyes of the past cannot comprehend the borderless world. And the language of the past is inadequate for developing a new dynamic. The first question is, how do you empower people in the situation of a new paradigm? We must begin with changing the language to help the process of empowerment. We should no longer talk about 'the rank and file' but about 'the front-line workers'. It seems an unfortunate expression. But he presses on. We must abandon the concept of 'hierarchy' and replace it with 'networks and fluidity'. Nothing should be 'imposed'. Instead, we should cultivate a 'feeling of ownership'. 'Control' belongs to an old paradigm. The new paradigm requires that we think, not of 'control' but of 'catalysation'. We should not talk about 'downsizing' but 'rightsizing'. Once, he says, we associated work with 'uniforms'; now we must think of 'multiforms'. The man in the front row nods his head. He understands all right. It's all part of human resource management. He might introduce the new concepts on the shop floor.

The speed with which the paradigm shift is taking place, the guru says, was well illustrated last month, when the chairman of Toyota speculated publicly about the future of the world car industry in the middle of the next century. How, with thinking like that going on, do we create a new paradigm for Australia? Again it comes back to the borderless world. The twenty-first century strategy requires an appreciation of the decline of the nation state and the rise of regions and cities—cities like Shanghai, Jakarta and Bombay. Australians should think in terms of regions to the north, but also to the west and east. Australia is multicultural with rich human resources and skills. Can you in Australia create ten Singapores? the guru asked rhetorically. The audience shuffles in its seats. No-one seems particularly keen. You have, he goes on, space and distance. These were once disadvantages, but they could in a new paradigm become advantages. You could look at the world with greater detachment, start from a zero base, and build a new paradigm of globalisation in a period of discontinuity. But first you must embark on the destruction of the old geopolitical architecture. Then work out where you can plug in, and exert leverage within new parameters.

The guru wound up his presentation with a joke. Like most guru jokes it was about the former Soviet Union. It was about a politician in Kazakhstan who began a speech by saying, 'Hands up all those in the audience who know what I'm going to say.' Half the audience put up their hands. 'Now hands up those who don't know what I'm going to say.' The other half put up their hands. 'Right,' said the politician, 'those in Group One who know what I'm going to say can explain it to the others in Group Two.' Then he bowed politely and left.

The guru did the same. He packed up his overheads like the

professor of economics, and walked out a door at the side of the rostrum. He had, it was said, to catch a plane. The audience stayed for coffee. Half of them were explaining the guru's words to the others. The man from the front row kept nodding his head and saying, 'Brilliant, brilliant.' It was, as someone pointed out, all a matter of communication.

Letters from the Fringe

You Are a Blundering Fool. Resign!

THOMAS CARLYLE kept all his letters and papers in a huge bath tub. An absent-minded man, he always knew then where things were. I've never had such a good system. I spend hours rummaging through cardboard boxes. The boxes contain the accumulated bric-a-brac of a life in politics. There are newspaper cuttings, reports on this and that, business cards from forgotten people, crumpled football records, monographed drink coasters, old passports and travel diaries, memos which seemed important at the time, and faded photographs. And letters. There are lots of letters.

I suspect we keep letters because they're more personal than other records. For better or worse people express themselves in letters. They put something into them. So my boxes contain lots of old letters. I doubt if I'd ever keep boxes of old faxes. They are somehow impersonal. People in love write passionate letters. I suppose it's possible to send a passionate fax. But I don't think it would be the same. When someone dies, or is ill, or suffers a misfortune, people write letters expressing compassion. I can't imagine a compassionate fax. Perhaps I'm suffering from 'high touch', a personal reaction to high technology. High touch is a real condition. It's why some people don't like leaving messages on telephone answering machines. It's why we go to movies when television and videos seem to make it unnecessary. I'm sure it's why we still write letters.

The old letter post of twenty or thirty years ago has given up a lot of ground to new technology. The telephone is used much more frequently. Businesses and increasingly individuals use the fax machine. But of the fifteen million articles handled by Australia Post each day, probably close to half are personal letters. At Christmas time there are a lot more.

Sorting out old letters is like walking down memory lane. People and events seem as they were at the time. They induce responses, smiles, sadness, deep sighs, anger and despair. They set you ruminating about the writer's motives and your own, about relationships, and what might have been if you'd chosen a different lifestyle or career.

The letter in my collection which intrigued me most came to me in New York. It had to be New York. I'd arrived there late at night and checked into my hotel. On the bed in my room there was a small, beautifully wrapped package. Inside the package there was a box. The box contained a solid gold ring with a big red ruby setting, and a letter in French on purple, scented, notepaper. It began, '*Mon cher, je t'aime toujours,*' and went on to say, 'Every time you come to New York I will be waiting for you.' There were more passionate declarations: a *billet doux* indeed. I stuck the jewel box and letter under my pillow and tried to go to sleep. People had told me about the excitement of New York, but this was too much. I imagined a beautiful Creole lady from Louisiana knocking gently on the door of my room. I slept badly. In the cold light of the following day I finally admitted the possibility that someone had made a terrible mistake. I took the ring and the letter to the hotel manager. He confirmed my suspicions. A lady was distraught. The manager was relieved and grateful. He sent a bottle of champagne to my room. This, I thought sadly, is the story of my life. I don't drink champagne.

Ministerial letters are sorted by a secretary but in opposition or as a backbencher you're pretty much on your own. In the old Parliament House, senators used to collect their mail from large boxes arranged like gym lockers in an area known euphemistically as the Club Room. In my second week as a politician I went into the Club Room to collect my mail. An elderly and long-serving senator had placed a large garbage container under his mail box and was scooping his mail straight into it. 'What are you doing that for?' I asked.

He looked at me like a sergeant major studying a new recruit. 'Son,' he said, 'when you've been here as long as I have you will understand that it's the only thing to do with this stuff.' He looked at me, observing my reaction, and decided to be more helpful. 'I'll give you a tip. Pick out a few occasionally and send them a telegram. It makes them think you're efficient.'

I was so shocked by this advice that I resolved to answer every letter I received. I tried to answer them politely although this was sometimes difficult. But they were all answered. Within weeks local government officials would find themselves receiving letters saying things like, 'Thank you for sending me a copy of the Southern Coast Water Board Annual Report, which I look forward to reading. I'm sorry that due to high interest charges the board has made a loss for the twenty-second year in a row. I hope next year will be better.'

Some letters, of course, couldn't be answered. They had no return address or arrived unsigned. I kept a lot of anonymous letters. I think it's because they threw up strange challenges and made you think about what might have been. I turned up one yellow with age that dated from 1984. Postmarked Surfers Paradise, written with a thumb nail dipped in tar and addressed to the minister for customs, it said simply, 'You are a blundering fool. Resign!' Why did I keep it? Maybe I thought the guy had something. But I've always wondered which particular aspect of my blundering foolishness provoked him to put thumb to paper. And what would have happened if I'd accepted his advice. I could have been blundering somewhere else. Perhaps writing letters to politicians from the Gold Coast.

Then there are the letters written in a slightly menacing tone. I kept them out of curiosity and a touch of nervous apprehension. How could you keep your confidence up when you get a letter saying, 'The real God knows your wickness [sic] and has decreed you fall. It will be sudden and without remedy'? And all this in an environment in which another correspondent wrote, 'I stay in my paddock. But I do know the REAL NAME OF GOD!!' It sounded like a minute from ASIO or the Department of Foreign Affairs. What hope do you have in a world of ignorance and terror?

Rummaging through boxes I found letters from people who clearly thought I didn't appreciate them enough: 'A sage only remistrates [sic] with a government three times. And then he must leave said country. Should I accept what Korea is offering me? One of the big three seats. My own school and the pick of the females. They understand someone of proven ability. And they want it.'

Nostalgia and xenophobia seem stronger emotions in letters written in the spindly handwriting of older people. I turned up letters that sighed for the 1950s and 1960s when Australia was an insulated place, and a well-kept secret. As one man summed it up: 'In the 1960s . . . we had not floated the dollar, we didn't have foreign banks, we didn't have Jap cars, we didn't have Jap whitegoods, etc, etc. It's about time the government got back to basics.' In pursuit of my early resolution I'd answer these letters and try and explain that the world had changed. Australia had to change too. But they were resilient correspondents, these people who treasured the past. They kept on writing, as if the country, like life itself, was ebbing away into an abyss. 'Wake up,' they'd say, 'before it is too late.' Some thought that for me it was already too late. 'What,' one asked, 'would your old headmaster think of you now? In my opinion you have failed the side badly. I am horrified that one with your background would even contemplate socialist ideals.'

Most of the old letters in the cardboard boxes were from caring people writing from the heart. Some were touching, a lot were thoughtful, and others very funny. It was the letters from the fringe which constantly reminded me that I'd ignored the advice of the old senator. I think he'd reached the point where he thought that all his letters were from confused or eccentric people. I didn't take his advice, but I decided early on that I should leave politics before I became like him.

The Strange Case of Hannah Prisk

In my ministerial office in Canberra there was a young woman called Tracey. She used to look through the mail before it was put on my desk, a service which I'd never had in my early days in politics. The old senator who threw all his letters in the bin might have appreciated Tracey. She was very good at her job. She divided the letters into bundles. She'd send all the formal bureaucratic letters to the department to prepare answers. Then she'd sort through the more personal ones and the ones she knew instinctively that I'd like to see. She'd give me a bunch of nice letters when I seemed depressed, and the nasty ones when I seemed happy. A short sharp rebuke like 'Why don't you shut your mouth?' signed 'Residents of South Yarra' is an example of a borderline case. Sometimes there could be no more depressing message for a member of parliament. Politicians are, after all, professional talkers. I didn't like such letters when I felt depressed. But when I was feeling good and Tracey presented me with this sort of document, I'd think, 'That's probably from a few stockbrokers having a drink in the Toorak Road Deli. We must be doing something right.'

There was a third category of letters: those which Tracey thought I might find challenging or intellectually stimulating, and to which I should give my personal attention. I received a letter like that in April 1991. I have kept it and some related correspondence. For me it remains a symbol of a peculiarly Australian, unresolved political problem. In fact in my own mind I've filed it away as 'The Strange Case of Hannah Prisk'. The letter read as follows:

> Dear Senator,
> I am the Hon. Secretary of the Yarram District Ladies Rugby Team. The girls and I are sick and tired of the assaults from under-employed Yallorn collery workers.
> Could you arrange for BHP—the big Australian, to develop a steel chastity belt for my girls?
> (Mrs) Hannah Prisk

At first sight, you might think this a quite ordinary letter. At the time I interpreted it differently. It seemed in such a few words to encompass so many issues. And it had a gutsy quality about it: the sort of letter that might have been written by one of the women who made Australia great. I wondered about Mrs Prisk. I rather liked her style. There were a couple of spelling mistakes. Perhaps, I thought, she's of European origin. Prisk sounded German to me but that was her husband's name. Hannah, too, might have been German. Later I was to find out she had a certain Teutonic thoroughness about her. But the thing I appreciated most was how she signed herself: '(Mrs) Hannah Prisk'. It had a nice formal precision about it. I could reply 'Dear Mrs Prisk' without any problem. I wouldn't have to decide whether to call her 'Ms' or 'Mrs' or 'Hannah'. Older people don't like 'Ms'. These days calling a woman you've never met by her Christian name is something of a risk. It can sound a bit 'fresh'. Anyway, it was the overall impression of Mrs Prisk's letter which got me interested.

Here she was, a married woman, giving her time voluntarily to an heroic cause. She was obviously outraged by the difficulties encountered by women entering a traditional all-male preserve. And yet there was a touch of compassion about her.

After all, the offenders were 'under-employed'. Idle hands make mischief. And in the last paragraph there was a cry from the heart, an appeal for the Big Australian, the flagship of national industry, to do something—an appeal with which in the old days I could identify.

For me personally, the letter had real poignancy. Deep down I felt that at last someone had understood what I meant by 'the productive culture'. Hannah Prisk clearly wanted local industry to solve her problem. She wanted to buy Australian. She wanted our industry to innovate, to develop new products where there might be a big market in the future. She was on my side. I responded accordingly:

> May I say how much I appreciate you writing to me about this matter. You will understand that for years I have tried to encourage industry to take a greater interest in community problems, and to encourage the community to take a keen interest in opportunities for industry. This may be my first big breakthrough.

I sent this reply as soon as possible. Deep down I knew that it wouldn't work. This sort of wimpish courtesy would not be sufficient for Mrs Prisk. She wanted action. I really didn't know what to do. To say I agonised over the problem would be exaggerating. But I did think about it. Finally I sent her letter with a covering note to Mr Brian Loton, the managing director of BHP. I knew that BHP wasn't interested in manufacturing small downstream products. I knew they'd think the market for steel chastity belts was too small. But I decided to give it a try. I'm afraid Mr Loton never wrote back. I guessed he was too busy at the time.

On the other hand, Mrs Prisk was not lacking in persistence. Another letter arrived:

> It is now over two weeks since I wrote you about the plight of the YLRT. I would remind you that Marie

> Neave, our half-back winger, once worked at the Boulevarde as a receptionist and her lips are not sealed. Anxiously awaiting your reply.
>
> I remain, (Mrs) Hannah Prisk

This, I thought, is a lady not to be messed with. She meant business. But Marie Neave had clearly got her facts wrong; she must have confused me with someone else. I couldn't recall having stayed at the Boulevarde. And yet I worried about it. Sometimes when you're distraught with the day's problems, feeling tired and emotional, one hotel seems just like another. I could have made a mistake. I wrote again to Mrs Prisk to tell her I was grappling with the problem. My letter didn't seem to reach her. She wrote again, on Anzac Day:

> I really do not know what you have to do to get a Ministerial reply. I suppose you have a team of alcoholic journos to do 'public relations' for you. The Ladies of Yarra Valley will not be polluted in this way. I am having afternoon tea with Mr Brian Loton, who is a real gentleman.
>
> In sorrow rather than anger, (Mrs) Hannah Prisk

Now I felt quite inadequate. Here was a woman forced into self help as a result of a failure of the political process. And her letter indicated a disappointed perception of politicians who were too busy or too lazy to deal with a quintessential Australian problem themselves.

I wrote back to Mrs Prisk. I wished her well with her afternoon tea and asked her to let me know how she got on. In the meantime I'd thought about suggesting martial arts training for the girls. It would help both with the rugby and the colliery workers. Maybe there was some relevant government funding available. I dithered about it. I was just afraid that Marie Neave and her teammates might take things too far. I imagined underemployed colliery workers with painful groin injuries. I didn't hear from Mrs Prisk again. I have never found out what happened. When I drive through the Yarra Valley I wonder about it all. The case remains an unsolved mystery.

I suppose that's why I kept the correspondence. Rereading it recently, I felt quite ashamed. In the last paragraph of my final letter to Hannah Prisk I wrote 'although we have not got any final solution to the problem facing your team, it is being worked on, and certainly we will get something in place for your girls before the next election.' Promises, promises. What a cop out. It's the sort of paragraph that could have been written by an alcoholic journalist who didn't care.

Pericoloso, Pistolet and Stench

In my filing cabinet there's a folder of old letters relating to one particular, unusual topic. They were sent to me at my Melbourne office during the time I was a minister. They arrived intermittently over a period of two or three years. At first I was puzzled by them, even slightly apprehensive. In fact, after I'd received two or three, I gave instructions that if any more arrived I'd open them myself. They would be identifiable by the handwriting and the European mode of address on the envelope: always 'Sig.', 'Herr' or 'M.'.

Opening them myself would mean that Tracey, my expert mail-sorter, would be free from any potential embarrassment. There would also be no chance of them falling into some bureaucratic in-tray. This possibility caused me some anxiety. The letters, I imagined, might be misinterpreted by some ambitious clerical assistant with low productivity and a vivid imagination. They might be passed on to ASIO or the federal police or some similarly inquisitive agency. Then anything could happen.

There used to be all sorts of rumours about ASIO. I didn't know whether to believe them or not. In the early eighties, when I was in opposition, I had a long talk with a senior ASIO officer at a social function. It was rather strange. During our discussion I remarked that I was 'sick to death of your guys bugging my phone. I'm not,' I said, 'asking you to do anything about it. You probably wouldn't anyway. I just want you to know that I've adopted a method of dealing with it myself. If I think a call is being bugged I just say to the caller, "I don't want to worry you, but I think ASIO is bugging our conversation. Don't take any notice. They've got a bunch of sexual deviants in there listening to conversations. They couldn't hold a job down anywhere else; they're too incompetent to understand what's important and what's not." '

The ASIO man gave me a chilling smile, bereft of any hint of amusement. 'Yes,' he said, 'I know you say that. They tell me about it.' It was probably some snoop technique to make me nervous. In a way it worked.

I spent quite some time trying to imagine who the writer of these letters could be, to construct a photokit of the author in my mind. I had only one clue: a page of a letter with a crossed-out PO box number in one corner, a PO box at a town on the central Queensland coast notorious as a watering hole for dole bludgers and retirees. There was nothing else. The letters kept coming from different addresses, signed with different names, but always in the same handwriting. Clearly the author travelled extensively and had a good knowledge of Europe and its languages. He was well-connected, frequenting gentlemen's clubs and, one suspected, the 'fleshpots' of various cities on the continent. His writing suggested a certain cavalier urbanity. Most significantly, he seemed to have an intimate knowledge of the workings of the international intelligence community, fortified, I suspected, by avid reading of spy fiction.

The best I could do with my photokit was a retired spook, bludging in the sun on the Queensland coast, a place chosen for its remoteness and the anonymity it offered. From time to time he made fleeting visits to Europe and Asia, or 'The Far East', as I'm sure he called it. These were sentimental visits to his past: always made on his terms. In the Queensland sun he'd write his strange letters to me, while his wife or lover did the crossword. Writing to me was a pastime which obviously amused him. It enabled him to recreate something of his past, and, at the same time, take the mickey out of a politician. Why he chose me I've never discovered. For a while I thought he might have been a distant relative or former lover of Mrs Hannah Prisk. In time I discounted this theory. He was not interested in social issues, only espionage.

When Gorbachev brought the Cold War to an end and the Berlin Wall was demolished, John Le Carré, the masterly writer of spy fiction, wrote an essay in which he mourned the consequences for his craft. He thought that the KGB would probably be dissolved. The CIA and MI6 would cut back their operations. Other intelligence agencies would suffer a similar fate. The essential constituents of good European espionage would be gone forever. There would be nothing to write about. Fortunately for Le Carré's readers his dismal forebodings turned out to be wrong. The scenes have shifted to places like the Middle East, Africa and Hong Kong, some of the players have changed, but the game goes on. And in more recent books like *Smiley's People* and *The Night Manager* Le Carré himself reveals that in 'the heart of darkness, the Whitehall intelligence community', it is business as usual.

In a sense I found this out for myself. My Queensland correspondent was clearly knowledgeable about these matters. In his own fanciful and elaborate construction of this environment, he made sure that the tentacles of the evil empire were reaching out to embrace me. I was to be involved in the shadowy world of attempted blackmail, bizarre facts and incompetent speculation which provide the daily bread of intelligence agencies and espionage writers. I was to be a pawn contributing to the entertainment of this nostalgic drop-out.

The first letter was written on the pale blue embossed notepaper of the Army and Navy Club, Pall Mall, situated, as I recall it, in the heart of Whitehall. It was postmarked 'Nice'. The letter was signed 'E. Pericoloso'. Meaning 'danger' in Italian, the word *pericoloso* was no doubt intended to encourage a sense of foreboding. Inside the envelope was a press clipping, a photo from a Melbourne newspaper of me sitting in the front row by a catwalk, watching a fashion parade. It seemed from the photo that I was gazing intently at the legs of the models dressed in beach wear. I remembered the fashion parade in question, and the photographer crawling on the floor to get this particular shot. His way of humanising a politician was by trying to turn him into a creep. The evil was in the lens of the camera. But I could see how the photo could be misrepresented. As soon as the clipping fell out of the envelope I sensed danger. In the letter Pericoloso told me that a copy of the press clipping had found its way into the hands of the mayor of Nice, who was in gaol on vice and corruption charges. The mayor, the letter went on, was 'very chuffed' to find out that an Australian minister was in 'the same line of business'. He believed it might help him with his defence. I would be advised of developments.

Pericoloso wrote again, this time from Bangkok. He informed me that the mayor of Nice was out on bail. The clipping of me had been stolen from him in gaol by a fellow prisoner who had subsequently escaped. This man, named Pistolet, was a deserter from the French Foreign Legion and had a criminal record. It was feared he might use the stolen clipping for some evil purpose. This information had been provided by French intelligence 'who are keenly interested in Pistolet'. Again I would be advised of any developments, probably by MI6. I heard nothing more from Pericoloso, apart from a short note to say he was being briefed at a safe house in the south of England. Pericoloso thought the agents at MI6 were 'incompetent' and had 'a black sense of humour'.

Inevitably a letter came from MI6 signed by a man called Stench ('Major: Retired'). The letter said that Stench was a code name. 'Six', the letter informed me, had developed an interest in Pistolet. And they had found out that he'd done a deal with the Marseilles police by volunteering for service in Djibouti with the French UN component. I wondered where this correspondence was leading. In a strange way, I'd become involved. For example, I developed a dislike of Major Stench. In his first few letters he seemed patronising and full of himself. He told me I should pass on the information to ASIO because 'frankly they take no notice of *us*'. In the same letter he warned me that ASIO was incompetent. I imagined him as being like the major in John Huston's film *Beat the Devil*—with a bowler hat, poison-tipped sword-cane, a clipped military moustache, and a mad gleam in his eyes. But as time passed I grew to like Stench better. His letters became more personal. He told me he lived with a woman called Moll, 'a great great grand-daughter of Moll Flanders'. He was clearly the master of a witty literary style. But then his news turned alarming. Pistolet had disappeared from Mogadishu. At the time he had been working on secondment in a US Army PX store. 'A period of some irregularities I understand—involving camels and American cigarettes.' The CIA was interested but also incompetent. 'Six', Stench wrote, thought Pistolet was heading for Australia. 'We are taking all measures to try and intercept him as he could be some embarrassment to your government. We still see the press clip as the key to his scheming.' The next communication was a hastily scrawled postcard:

> I have a disconcerting piece of news. Something about a plot to blow up the House (Parliament, not yours). Will try and confirm so you can warn ASIO. This from the French courtesy Mossad. May be another Guy Fawkes lark, but you never know.
>
> PS A. Blunt sends warm regards. Stench.

A few weeks later an envelope arrived, postmarked Singapore. It contained a small white card. It said simply:

> A bas les War Lords D'eritrea
> Vive 'Le One Nation' et le Grenadier Keatinge
> Avec mes respects profounds, Pistolet.

I had become engrossed by these developments. I turned the card over and over with a trembling hand. I was contemplating leaving politics. I finally accepted that Pistolet was coming. Maybe it was a hint that it was time to go.

When the inevitable letter arrived I knew at once—from its blackmailing character, its self-pity, and its obsequiousness—who it was from.

> Signor, my good friend Chevalier Stench has suggested that I ask you to sponsor me for Australian citizenship. I am a refugee, you see, from the French Intelligence, from the Foreign Legion (I served with distinction in the Casbah at Sidi Bel Abbas, but circumstances obliged me to leave before my colour service expired) and from the Marseilles Police Department on some trumped-up charge, and now from the mayor of Nice, who you may have heard has bribed his way out of gaol and accuses me of unsanitary practices and other forms of malfeasance. I am innocent, Signor. I wish only to be part of one nation and, qui sait?, perhaps lend my talents to the great cabinet of distinguished men who command the resources of that nation.

And then came the blackmail bit: 'If you will sponsor me I shall, of course, destroy the photographs taken by my Singapore friends in your room at The Oriental. You are a proud man, Signor, very proud. *Ca alors, une exposition vraiment incroyable.*'

The letter contained several swipes at Stench, describing him as 'an unsavoury character', and went on:

> Alas the Chevalier is not the man he was: not very proud, and not very often. Let me say, however, as one Boulevardier to another, that I do not find it surprising that a man so proud as you, should have had, shall we say, a certain past. But my lips are sealed and the photographs will be destroyed, if all goes well, hein?

Remember me in your prayers, Excellency.
Your obedient servant, Pistolet

In this man, Pistolet, my imaginative correspondent had clearly created a monster. I felt quite disgusted by him. But, of course, there was nothing I could do. So I did nothing. The last thing I heard was in a short letter from Major Stench: 'Pistolet still concerns me. I suppose you know he made it to Australia, but has been deported by those idiotic toads in your Immigration Department, who thought he was a Serb.'

With hindsight the whole business seems far-fetched. But thumbing through my file I found a letter from Pericoloso, which used those very same words: 'This may seem far-fetched, but I assure you anything can happen on the Cote D'Azur'. As for the author of all these letters, I imagine him claiming damages from MI6 for discharging him with a split personality, a condition arising from his former profession. Or, maybe, he's just laughing to himself in the Queensland sun. Perhaps his past caught up with him and he met a terrible fate.

Documating Troublems

Everyone has views about politicians, most of them, like Hannah Prisk's, none too charitable. Usually it's their public faces which are not liked. They seem so predictable and messy, with conditioned reflexes and survival skills. You know precisely what they're going to say before they open their mouths. But scratch the thick skin of some politicians and underneath you find a hidden talent. I always thought Bob Hawke was good at doodling and sketching faces. He used to do it in cabinet, to while away the late night hours, when the minds turned to bubble gum, as Paul Keating used to say. Gareth Evans I remember, could turn in a mean performance in a karaoke bar in Tokyo, but that was an intangible talent, which with his natural diplomacy he exercised overseas.

I kept Hawke's drawings and doodles: maybe I'm a closet archivist, with a quirky sense of history. I found them recently in a box of old papers and documents. In the box there was a fat bundle of notes on cabinet letterhead, cards and scraps of paper. They were written by John Kerin, the tall, genial man in the broad-brimmed hat who'd been a minister in the Hawke and Keating governments. Kerin understood country people, and knew most of what there was to know about rural industries. People sensed this and respected him for it.

I showed Kerin's notes to a friend. 'These,' she said, 'are postcards from the ledge.' The cards and letters reminded me that John Kerin was a homespun intellectual and a sardonic observer of human affairs. He was sceptical and irreverent—a huge political disability.

As the British politician Richard Crossman pointed out in his *Diaries*, cabinet government is a tortuous exercise in group therapy. Some ministers talk a lot, and others hardly talk at all. Some read the ubiquitous cabinet papers over and over, and some do crosswords. Kerin was not a prolific talker. He didn't keep a diary. He wrote notes in which he debated issues, commented on events and people, and recorded the foibles of politics and government. He was in his own way a chronicler of his times. I'm glad I kept his notes. Unofficial histories are much less boring.

The intellectual bit was reflected in an inquiring mind. 'Button,' he wrote, 'what's this bloody "forex" market Keating keeps talking about? When I was young Forex was the name of a French letter.'

'Why,' he asked, 'do you allow yourself to be intimidated by Sister Ryan, and state that affirmative action is OK? What we'll end up with is a situation like New York where police have equal rights, and hence you have a white, a black and a Hispanic, male or female, all midgets, who have to travel in threes to survive?'

He was suspicious of political jargon. A note defined the jargon of the mid-eighties:

Euphemisms
structural adjustment = go broke slowly
adjustment = go broke quickly
managed change = the bastards keep you on the rack
high tech = subsidise multinationals
European Unity = fewer tanks in the street.

When the future of the Antarctic was discussed Barry Jones argued for more money for research. 'The Antarctic,' he said, 'is in particularly bad shape.' Kerin attributed this to other things. 'This is due to (1) the wage freeze? (2) Keating's cold heart? (3) the weather? (4) the continental drift?' The Cape York Spaceport proposal produced a note of inquiry: 'Will this put us into the 21st Century? If we can find a desolate site, will any trees have to be killed? Have you checked for lizards? If it creates wealth and jobs in a non-inhabited area, will opposition have to be marshalled in Sydney and Melbourne?'

The homespun part came from a sensitivity to the bush and his political constituency: 'Farmers are beaut people—philanthropic, altruistic, and with a strong streak of humanity. But if we give them a capital gains tax, quarantine farm losses and don't change the assets test, I'll be living in a Mayne Nickless truck with gun slots for windows.' He complained that his views were often misinterpreted because he had 'to deal with the sons of the disappearing soil', who were cautious about change. 'This proposal,' he once wrote, 'should cause enough chaos to be regarded as a major reform.'

The consideration of tax file numbers was a two-edged sword. 'Dr G. Edelsten will head up an agency to guarantee that no-one escapes paying his dues to society. Only one group of Australians will get off scot free. This group comprises businessmen, cockies, rock singers, wogs, illegal residents and pot growers.' Often decisions of the government seemed more positive. 'I'm now fully armed for my task of persuading wheat cockies, railway workers, sugar mill workers and coal miners of the path of economic rectitude. "Reform and repent. Reconstruct or die," I'll be saying from now on.'

I first became aware of his propensity for note-writing in 1982. We were both touring electorates in north and central Queensland. We met up one night at a meeting in a public hall in the town of Bowen. There were salads and bits of chicken and cakes and a sprightly old lady playing a piano which seemed more waterlogged than the one in the film. She played 'The Bonnie Banks of Loch Lomond' and 'The Road to the Isles' and later 'Now is the Hour'. In the meantime John Kerin made a speech. He told jokes interspersed with serious bits. There were, he said, many 'troublems'. They had to be analysed and then 'documated' before action could be taken. The audience thought it was good stuff. Later I chided him about his mixing up of words. In the morning there was a note under the door of my motel room:

> If your troublems get you beat
> Documate and they'll be sweet.

From then on I suppose I encouraged him. But when he left politics in 1993 I feared a gap in the unofficial history. There may be too many people saying merely predictable things. I nearly lost him as a chronicler of events in 1985. 'Your selective leaking of some of our personal correspondence has caused me some troublems. Therefore, regardless of my factitiousness, cynicism, pessimism and occasionally suicidal approach to government, this is the last bloody note you'll get.' But the notes kept coming. He was addicted. He handed them out like a bookie's clerk. Other people have their own collections. What might have been a political diary of substance is scattered to the four winds. The troublem is he never had a feel for the earnestness of being important. And he didn't documate it with sufficient care.

Suspect PM Clinically Insane

I put my copy of Alan Clark's *Diaries* on the table in front of me, and sat back to enjoy my cappuccino. Steaming hot coffee makes my reading glasses mist up. I thought I'd take a break for a minute or two. A tweedy, but pleasant-looking, middle-aged Englishwoman and her husband were sitting at the next table. Academics I guessed. She looked over at my book. 'Women don't like him,' she pronounced.

'Is that so?' I asked. 'I think the problem is that they do. Too many of them.'

'He's very chauvinist,' she said.

I sensed the discussion might develop into a silly argument, a waste of time in Harry's Bar in Venice. It seemed an odd venue in which to 'dig in' defending Alan Clark, a Conservative British politician. I decided on a tactical retreat. 'Yes,' I said. 'He is a chauvinist.'

It's hard to know why people keep detailed diaries. If they keep them for close friends or family they're a bit like letters: records of events thought to be interesting. If they keep them for a wider audience, or perhaps for posterity, they become like newspaper articles or history books. For a politician, keeping a diary requires patience, discipline and time. In public life the discipline is needed in the ordering of priorities. Recording events becomes as important as participating in them. It's an egocentric pastime. Because it is a contemporaneous record it probably produces a more accurate account. But finding the time is not easy.

Peter Howson, a minister of the Menzies era, published *The Howson Diaries* in 1984. I can't recall any other Australian politician who has attempted this feat, though Neal Blewett, a minister in the Hawke and Keating governments, threatens to do so. He is patient, disciplined and an historian. These are the right qualifications. With luck he won't start a vogue amongst those who don't have them. Without the qualifications or temperament to keep a full record of events I used to write spasmodic notes on bits of paper or in my pocket diary. Things like 'suspect PM clinically insane', 'minister X is a terrible wimp' or 'Y is a misanthropic thug'. They're useful as aides memoire.

Richard Crossman's *The Diaries of a Cabinet Minister* are perhaps the most famous political diaries of the postwar period. Crossman was a scholar, and one-time editor of the *New Statesman*, who turned up as a senior minister in the Harold Wilson government between 1964 and 1970. Described as 'one of those meteors that occasionally lighten the British political firmament', he endured all the discomforts of the intellectual in politics. He wrote many of his diary entries during cabinet meetings. This made his colleagues ill at ease. They hated him for it. In his early writings, and as a minister, Crossman wrestled with the problem of to what degree British parliamentary democracy is 'a sham, a fraud or a hoax'. He believed in open government. He made records of day-to-day events in cabinet, and their ultimate publication raised the 'tut tut' disapproval of the political establishment. He regarded his diaries as his greatest contribution to British political life.

Crossman did not suffer fools gladly, and once described an important government report as a 'fascinating exposition of civil service stoogery and idiocy'. He described his relationship with civil servants as follows: 'When I am in a good mood they occasionally allow an ordinary human being to come and visit me; but they make sure that I behave right and that the other person behaves right; and they know how to handle me . . . Yes Minister, No Minister, If you wish it Minister.' This is where it all began for Sir Humphrey Appleby and the rest of the cast of *Yes Minister.*

Alan Clark may not be well known in Australia. He was a Conservative member of the House of Commons from 1974 to 1992. He was not particularly interested in the fine points of parliamentary democracy. He 'did time', as he might put it, as minister for employment, then trade and finally defence in

Margaret Thatcher's government, and then briefly under John Major. Between 1983 and 1992 he kept an interesting, and vastly entertaining diary, which he published in 1993. Metaphorically speaking, no expletives have been deleted.

Clark is a wealthy English gentleman. He lives in a magnificent-looking castle in the south of England, called 'Saltwood'. Once a year he has a 'traditional' swim in the moat. In Scotland the rolling acres of his property, Eriboll, sweep down in a Gaelic panorama to a loch. There's a ski chalet at Zermatt in Switzerland. He has about a dozen cars at Saltwood, including six vintage Jaguars, a Porsche, two Citroëns, 'for holidays', and a Rolls Royce Silver Ghost, 'the nicest of all to drive on a fine day'. So there is a lifestyle which constantly competes with his fascination for politics: a competition which resulted in his not making the most of either. In 1983, following the election, he was set for the ministry, but he couldn't make up his mind whether he wanted a job or not. When he became minister for employment he describes how his new secretary 'made plain her feelings on several counts: (1) I am an uncouth chauvinist lout; (2) that it is a complete mystery why I have been made a minister; (3) that my tenure in this post is likely to be a matter of weeks rather than months'.

In fact, Clark lasted as employment minister for three years, and was bored to death. He wanted more action and hankered after the jobs of the secretary of state for defence and the foreign secretary. He never made it to either position.

Clark's *Diaries* are very funny, honest and revealing. He's a sort of modern-day Samuel Pepys, with an up-market James Bond recklessness and polish. His ambitions, lusts and prejudices are faithfully recorded. He has 'the hots' for a red-headed telephonist, and falls 'madly in love' with the Labour candidate opposing him in his constituency. Chevenement, the French defence minister, is 'odious, rude, uncouth and objectionable'. High-powered international meetings are 'extraordinarily draining and repetitious', and 'the French, shits as always'. His colleagues come in for the same treatment. He speculates and plots his political future, seemingly obstructed by his 'loathsomely conspiring' namesake, Kenneth Clarke, destined to become the chancellor of the exchequer. His ambition can only be achieved 'if Clarke has a nervous breakdown—unlikely in one so fat—or—perfectly possible at any time, he must make the Norwich Union wince—something "happens" to him. One mustn't be uncharitable (why not?) but this is, after all, the roughest game, at the biggest table.'

The James Bond bit comes from his macho competitiveness, his constant philandering and the lifestyle symbols of cars, good wine, clubs and calculated boredom. He gives a party and laments being down three bottles of Dom Perignon, three Talbot Blanc, four 78 Morgan and so on. Climbing a mountain in France, he has to beat another unknown climber, ascending the same slope. He celebrates an election victory lunching with 'the coven', three women whom he'd known for many years, and afterwards they drive past the Ritz. 'I wish we could go in there,' one of the women remarks. 'Why?' asks Clark. 'To go to bed, of course,' she tells him. 'I was thoughtful,' says Clark. 'I have always been culpably weak in such matters.'

My former colleague Michael Duffy used to run into Clark at international meetings when they were both trade ministers. Cruising across Lake Constance on a ferry one night, on the way to a conference, they listened to Martin Bangermann, a plump and ebullient German politician, wax lyrical through a microphone about the beauties of the lake. 'I can't see a thing. Doesn't this idiot realise it's pitch black?' Clark remarked to the assembled ministers. It seems that he was ever so. Duffy, also susceptible to boredom, says, 'I always liked to sit next to him on a bus.'

Clark visited Canberra in 1988. Before we met I tried to find out more about him in the library. There was a profile from the *Spectator*. He sounded capable, outspoken and a little eccentric. It claimed that prior to his entry into politics there was no evidence of his ever having worked. This seemed unfair. He had written several notable books on military history. The article referred to one of his more notorious exploits: eloping with a sixteen-year-old girl from a convent. They were subsequently married, and he took her for their honeymoon on a tour of war graves in France. I wondered what to expect. At dinner he was witty, acerbic and irreverent. He was on his way to Japan. He doubted if the British would ever be able to compete with the Japanese, unless there was a more level playing field. He thought the solution might be to level the playing field by introducing fast-food chains into Japan as quickly as possible. Junk food would ruin the Japanese diet, undermine their alertness and morale, and produce a rapid decline in productivity. I'm sure he had similar solutions for dealing with most countries, but perhaps no solutions for Britain.

In his *Diaries*, referring to his time as a minister, Clark describes himself as a 'privileged prisoner'. It's a compelling and accurate description of what ministerial life can be like: particularly for a man of his temperament, eclectic taste and zany humour. But perhaps it was the prison-like detachment which enabled him to write the *Diaries*. He doesn't seek approval: only insights which he shares with gay abandon. The resulting book has been described as malicious, lecherous, self-pitying, 'staggeringly, recklessly candid'. Political diaries must run the risk of being burdened with the lifeless mechanics of politics: and political autobiographies are frequently self-serving. Clark manages to escape these traps. He captures the excitement, the pettiness, the mania and the boredom of professional politics with a sharp and sardonic prose. He sees the funny side of most things, including himself, and reveals in an exchange with a parliamentary colleague, preoccupied with Britain's inflation rate, why he was never destined for the political heights: 'Personally I wonder if it matters all that much. It's a million per cent or whatever in Brazil, and you can still get taxis and delicious meals. Sex doesn't stop.' How's that for being politically incorrect?

Reading Kinky

Whatever the orthodoxy of the time, it seems heretical for a politician to be politically incorrect. Like letting the side down. Comedians, impersonators and satirists are not PC by nature. Incorrectness is part of their art. They make people laugh at pomposity and self importance. This is refreshing. It even makes people feel better.

A friend often consults me about his health. He thinks I'm a good listener, and he knows I don't charge. Doctors sometimes tell him things he doesn't want to hear. He suspects their diagnostic techniques, and often contemplates second opinions, or putting his health business out to tender. He is a frequent traveller overseas. On long flights he used to worry about his blood pressure or cholesterol level. More recently he's been trying to think about other things. On his second last overseas trip he offered fifteen different Singapore Airlines flight attendants jobs in his office. It sounded like an attractive fantasy, but it is high risk. It might send his blood pressure up. I recommended the crime writer Kinky Friedman as a suitable and engaging diversion. In India, my friend asked for Kinky Friedman books in a number of shops. 'No sah,' they kept telling him, 'Mr Kinky Friedman, he is not here in India.' He sent me a postcard from India telling me the sad news. It seemed an important piece of information. The sort of thing you mightn't find browsing on the Internet.

Kinky Friedman is in New York and his books are here in Australia, including a volume called *Kinky Friedman Crime Club*. I can imagine it being diverting on long flights. The man himself is a country and western singer with a band called The Texas Jewboys. Everything about him is politically incorrect. Recently he turned to writing detective stories. His stories have convoluted and dubious plots, but get by with a series of wicked one-liners. There are no ancient aphorisms of the 'Too many cooks spoil the broth' kind. Instead he points out that 'if Moses had been a committee, the Jews would probably have never gotten out of Egypt'. He knows a 'hotshot lawyer, who once got a charge of sodomy reduced to following too closely'. In bed with his girlfriend Uptown Jane, he is interrupted by the telephone, 'I'll call back,' he snaps, 'I'm in the middle of someone.'

Wearing his private detective hat, Friedman lives with his cat in the attic loft of a grey graffiti-strewn warehouse in Greenwich Village. The loft is as 'cold as hell . . . depending on the season in hell'. From nearby he hears the rhythmic thuddings of a lesbian dance class. The loft is his sanctuary. Its principal furnishings are an espresso machine, two telephones and a bull's horn, from which he discharges whisky into his mouth 'like Ernest Hemingway's shotgun'. He is an inveterate cigar smoker. From the window of the loft he looks out on the smoggy nightmare of New York, and a streetscape of garbage trucks and low life. He's not a tough guy and doesn't carry a gun. He merely contemplates the tough life. He thinks it is things like 'ordering from a wine list'. If there's heavy business to be done he relies on Boris, a large Russian strangler expert in martial arts. A highly contemporary New Yorker, Kinky thrives on coffee, sexual fantasies, cigars, 'power naps', whisky and wisecracks.

New York Jewish humourists have been so pervasive that it's hard to remember if America has produced any other kind since Mark Twain. The line runs from Dorothy Parker and the Marx Brothers to Mort Sahl and Woody Allen. Now Kinky Friedman is emerging as a new cult figure. He's less into interpersonal relationships than Woody Allen. In fact he doesn't have any. His scepticism is street-smart. His friendships are transitory, apart from a loyal Dr Watson-type follower called Ratso. He skirts the edges of the New York drug culture, frequents the bars of the Village and the eating houses in Canal Street, and returns to his loft to think through the complexities of bizarre crimes with his cat. As a private eye he doesn't seem to get paid. There are hints that he remains a musician, falling into the world of crime as he tries to find a lost cat, clear a wrongly accused reporter, or help out some musician friends at the Lone Star Cafe.

Friedman will inevitably become identified with New York. He reflects its seediness, its cynicism and its neuroticism, but rarely its magic. His humour is pure New York. Great cities seem to embrace crime fiction as part of their culture. London has done it since Sherlock Holmes, Paris did it with Simenon, Los Angeles with Raymond Chandler, Chicago with Sara Paretsky. In Australia Peter Corris has had a go at it in Sydney, and Shane Maloney in Melbourne. Like cats crime writers seem to identify with places. When they move away from places which they know, and love, they tend to lose their touch.

Chandler is said to have created Los Angeles as a literary entity. He remains the most lasting and famous exponent of the tough guy school of crime fiction. He was a highly literate intellectual who defended the art of mystery writing against the 'parvenu insecurity' of literary critics and writers of 'social significance twaddle'. His private eye Philip Marlowe became a cult hero. A British professor of literature invited to address the San Francisco 'Marlowe Society' was surprised to find his audience interested in Philip but not Christopher. Chandler had a strong relationship with his hero Marlowe, who shared some of his own social values: it was as if they were friends. 'Marlowe and I,' he once wrote, 'do not despise the rich because they take baths and have money: we despise them because they are phoney.' Friedman is sometimes described as a writer in the Chandler mould. He's not. He's a gag man masquerading as a crime writer. One suspects it's all tongue in cheek. No one could take him seriously. I'm sure he laughs a lot at his own jokes, which seems reasonable. They are funny.

The problem with my friend is that he laughs a lot, with a great deal of exuberance. Reading Kinky Friedman on a plane would probably mean he'd have to be shifted to a designated laughing seat, so that he wouldn't upset the other passengers. He might develop a stitch, which in an anxious moment he could misinterpret as a heart attack or a serious stomach complaint. He once overdosed on Vitamin B tablets, and could overdose again with Kinky. I have recommended that he give it a try, assessing his symptoms as he goes. Some books, like drugs, should be taken with moderation.

Talking Politics

The Correct Question

I SUPPOSE it's a bad habit. I walk into somebody's house, exchange greetings, and before I realise it I'm browsing through the books on the nearest shelf. The temptation seems irresistible. Books tell you something about the occupants of the house: what their interests are, their favourite recreations, and perhaps their views about life. A TV flickering in the corner of the room, or a computer, tell you nothing. A private video library might indicate something. But I don't know anybody with a private video library and, in any event, the covers of videos are not very helpful.

Some people have only a very small bookshelf, containing things like an old *Pictorial Atlas of Australia*, a Jeffrey Archer novel purchased at an airport, a school dictionary, and a few bound volumes of early copies of *National Geographic*. There's not much conversational mileage in a bookshelf like that. You look around for a drink and a plate of pretzels instead.

I found myself delving again into a friend's bookshelf a few weeks ago. There were handsome books on art and design, and an array of the latest literary bestsellers. It was all very contemporary and interesting. Then, tucked away in the middle of it all, I found a set of six little volumes, old, but well cared for. They were the stories of Little Black Sambo, Little Black Bobtail, Little Black Mingo and the rest of their gang. I glanced surreptitiously over my shoulder at the other more socially adept guests. They were engrossed in the burble of conversation over pre-dinner drinks. I flipped through the books one by one. I wondered what they were doing in this bookshelf. I could remember the days when they were regarded as so politically incorrect as to be almost subversive.

The Little Black Sambo books were first published in 1901. It might be argued that they reflect the patrician attitudes of the Victorian missionary era. In fact, they're gentle little stories counselling about the risks involved in trusting tigers or lighting matches near drums of kerosene, and suggesting the rewards which follow from being nice to your mum. But for a while they went quite out of fashion because Little Black Sambo was black. It's even been suggested that Noddy went out of fashion because some people thought that Noddy and Big Ears were gay.

Official morality has always had an influence on approved literary taste. In the 1960s, according to John Mortimer, a book was found by the courts to be 'depraving and corrupt if it caused its readers to slaver at the mouth, walk with their knuckles brushing the ground, and show a general tendency to breathe heavily'. Quite a few books, like *Lady Chatterley's Lover* and most of Henry Miller, fell into this category. On my first visit to England a copy of *Tropic of Cancer*, bought in Rome in the shadow of the Vatican, but banned in the UK and Australia, was taken from me at the Dover ferry terminal. 'Something in your pocket, sir,' said one of those incredibly polite plainclothes constables as I walked happily out of the Customs Hall. I froze on the spot, tried to regulate my breathing, put one hand in the air, and wiped my mouth with the back of the other. But it was too late. No wonder I delved into Little Black Sambo with caution.

In the late 1950s the first film depicting distant nudity was shown in Australia. Called *One Summer of Happiness*, it was artfully promoted with the advice that 'the nude bathing scenes are absolutely inoffensive'. Provided with this convenient alibi, people rushed to see it. What more politically correct position could there be than sitting in judgment on the film oneself.

There is a certain Anglo-Saxon irony in the fact that in America 'PC' means political correctness and in England it means police constable. Political correctness is a fashion which should never be allowed to become a habit. 'Black', for example, a pejorative expression for one generation of whites, gave way to 'Black is Beautiful', a declaration of black pride and dignity. Sexist jokes, directed solely against women, were offensive to the idea of sexual equality. Now that they are directed as much at men as women, the balance is being redressed. There are so many jokes around about nationality as distinct from race that the joke books are probably in a state of equilibrium. On the other hand ageist jokes seem to remain predominantly against the old, and sizeist jokes about the small. I've always been in one category and am progressively getting into the other. If a backlash movement develops against this sort of humour, I want to join. But I won't be advocating a ban.

In this country 'White Australia' was politically correct for most of our history. Australia was sustained by the 'Empire', and threatened by malign outside influences like the 'Yellow Peril' and the 'Communist Octopus'. Confronted by the facts and some enlightened political leadership these bogies went out of fashion. More recently feminism and multiculturalism have become politically correct. They are concepts which are at the same time increasingly difficult to define. Changes to their style and content seem inevitable. A recent survey of teenage Australians, conducted by the Australian Commission for the Future, revealed some distaste for multiculturalism. They thought it a useful word and politically correct, but whatever their racial origin they didn't like it much. Perhaps it had become too PC. Long-serving governments, like the Hawke–Keating government, establish an ambience in which their idea of political correctness tends to prevail. Inevitably there is a backlash. In time a new PC environment will develop in its place.

Sometimes well-meaning pressure is applied to governments to legislate against intolerance and stupidity. This sort of pressure resulted in our racial vilification law. Spokespeople for some ethnic communities thought it a good idea. It was something special for them. There is, however, a large grey area between offensive racism and the swapping of mild invective. Defining the rules is not easy. It's hard to work out if a comment like 'I won't work with him, he's a bloody whingeing Pom' is discrimination in employment, racial vilification, or just part of our culture. It is a nice point as to whether intolerant social behaviour can be fixed by legislation. The danger is in creating a legislative steamroller to crack a few nuts.

The most worrying thing about the racial vilification law is the arguments which were advanced in favour of it. We were told that it was needed in Australia because of the rise of racially motivated vilification and violence in Germany, France and Italy. It was as if the manifestation of racial intolerance was a disease like Asian Flu, Delhi Belly or German Measles which spreads across borders and continents, irrespective of history, environment, or immune systems. It was said that many states in America have legislation of this kind, and therefore we should have it too. There was not much analysis of whether it works to reduce racial tension in a country which seems to have a much bigger problem than us. Existing laws, it was said, were inadequate to deal with possible contingencies. The passing of legislation would reduce anxiety and apprehension amongst minority groups.

Despairing of publicly articulated arguments of this kind, I asked a sensible lawyer whether he favoured legislation. He told me he knew a Chinese girl, a visiting student, who'd been asked by a man in the street in Sydney if she was an Australian citizen. When she replied, 'No,' the man said, 'Well in that case you ought to go back to China.' This seems more like stupidity and ignorance than racial vilification. It's hard to legislate against stupidity. Yet my lawyer friend saw this incident as a justification for legislative action. Lawyers sometimes have a touching faith in the value of the written law.

Before the racial vilification law was passed, the Australian statute books already contained a host of remedies to deal with problems involving behaviour which is offensive to other citizens. There are laws relating to unlawful assembly, incitement, damage to property, indecent language, defamation, libel, assault, obscenity, and offensive behaviour. Some of them have fallen into partial disuse but they are still there. The great thing about them is that, in theory at least, they apply equally to all citizens: to men and women, to young people and old people, to black and white, to people of all racial origins and religious beliefs. There is no special category of citizens to be treated differently under these old laws. And the moods and fashions and attitudes of the community will always reinforce the way in which the law is administered.

Community attitudes are in constant change. It's not so long ago that magistrate's courts were cluttered with men charged with using indecent language. Listening to today's schoolgirls at a bus stop is sometimes a reminder that their grandfathers would have been locked up for using the same language. A few years ago the word 'wog' was used with strong pejorative connotations. Today it is used with little animosity and even some affection. It has been adopted by some ethnic communities as useful slang.

Pegging out the borderline of tolerable behaviour is not easy. An Australian Chinese friend once described to me an occasion when he was travelling on a tram in Melbourne. A man sitting opposite him, an old digger type, leaned forward and said, 'How ya goin', dim sim?' The Chinese, a polite and astute man replied, 'Very well thank you. How about you, kangaroo tail soup?' The Australian spent the rest of the ride explaining why he'd never liked kangaroo tail soup. The Chinese man felt good about the incident.

All this seems pretty innocuous stuff which might, in most circumstances, be called harmless banter. It's within the limits of tolerance, and a lot of it probably goes on. It is to be expected in a multiracial society like Australia, which has people from 260 nationalities amongst its population. We have reason to be proud of the relative ease with which this country has accommodated the seeming eccentricities of various migrant groups. The absorption of migrants from various nationalities into the community is an Australian success story. Perhaps it stems from an easy-going tolerance and friendliness. Perhaps Australians recognise that, with the arguable exception of the Aboriginal people, we are all migrants or descendants of migrants and a lot of people have worked hard at making it a success. We've come a long way from the primitive racism of a White Australia policy.

PC is like beer, best taken in moderation, and preferably mild rather than bitter. Otherwise it develops its own dour bureaucracies where ideas are institutionalised in filing cabinets of the mind. It threatens the natural evolution and extension of the English language with phoney made-up words. PC challenges critical intelligence with dubious dogmas. It tends to rewrite history so that we pretend things didn't happen when they did. That seems a strange thing to do in the name of progress. It is surely better to recognise that people used to think in particular ways about race, colour, sexual preference, gender and so on, but are now better informed about these issues, and more tolerant and sensitive to inequalities. Or so we like to think.

I suppose every country has its share of people naturally addicted to PC. Australia is no exception. Our PC trends were, however, imported, mostly from international bureaucratic organisations or countries with different and sometimes confused social values like America. Australians fortunately have their own unique scepticism, humour and sense of fairness to filter the sensible from the ridiculous and humane values from bureaucratic ones.

A world in which political correctness became a habit rather than a passing fashion would be potentially grey and humourless, and ultimately intolerant. I can't imagine a world without jokes or anecdotes about differences of race, class, nationality, sex, age or size. I don't want to. I like the freedom to judge some humour as tasteless, cruel, intolerant or unfair. We should all be able to make judgments about that, indulging our own private little models of political correctness. It's the imposed model of the self-appointed thought PCs, as the British understand the term, which should be rejected as a habit.

On my own bookshelf I have a book printed in German. Its title on the cover is *Proceedings of the 20th Party Congress of the Communist Party of the Soviet Union.* Inside, however, is the text of Wolfgang Leonard's work *The Revolution Gives Up Its Children,* a critique of the Soviet system. The book was produced that way, long before the Berlin Wall came down, so that East Germans could read it on trains and in other public places. It was a device to help people avoid the intrusion and persecution of a repressive regime. It is a reminder of a society where political correctness was taken to extremes.

Sitting on the Fence with an Ear to the Ground

I haven't been to Canberra much since 1993. Before that I overdosed. The second time I went back I had a cup of morning coffee in a little shop in the Civic Centre. It seemed peaceful, like a country town. Then I went up to Parliament House which exudes its own extraordinary background hubbub. It reminded me of the distant roar from the Melbourne Cricket Ground on the day of a big match. The sound mostly comes from the TV monitors and audio systems in all the offices where apparatchiks keep an eye and an ear on what's happening in the chambers. Parliament House is a high-tech building: believe it or not, it's what architects call an 'intelligent' building. Making the transition from Canberra's Civic Centre to Parliament House feels like being in a jumbo jet that's just hit a patch of turbulent air. The vibrations and shuddering are a bit alarming.

In the chambers themselves, if you close your eyes for a minute, the noise has a different and distinct quality. It sounds like amateur fishermen swapping insults in a crowded pub.

'You told a whopper last year.'

'Sure mate, I told a whopper, but it was a different sort of season, and it wasn't as big as the whopper you told.'

The language in a budget session is the most extravagant. It's rich with synthetic outrage, stimulated by the day's newspapers and the morning radio. There is plenty of mud-slinging, but not much technocratic jargon. That's kept for the electorate. A lot of politicians think a bit of technical stuff helps them sound expert. Parliament, however, is intolerant of obtuse language.

There is a charitable and sensible view of parliament as a form of theatre. According to this view, the real work of politicians and government goes on behind the scenes, in committees, party meetings and cabinet. Parliament allows the passions to rage. Winston Churchill thought it was a terrible system, but he couldn't think of a better one. Paul Keating understood the theatre of politics. Parliament as theatre becomes a medieval jousting tournament, or a bull ring where you goad your opponents, stick barbs into them and weaken their resolve. Sometimes the barbs are too sharp, and the wider audience gets upset. They think it's a bit rich.

Keating saw it as an arena of combat: 'I'm in the grenade-throwing business; occasionally I drop one beside my foot, but I get many direct hits.' Mostly he sensed the mood, playing Iago, Polonius or Macbeth as the occasion demanded. He could hear the applause of the crowd in the pit—but not the silence in the dress circle. Australia, a lucky country, is mostly dress circle. The most interesting politicians of the last few decades have had a thespian quality about them: Menzies, Hawke, Whitlam and Keating. Others like Mick Young, Jim McLelland, Jim Killen and Barry Jones used their wit to great effect. Whitlam and Keating had both theatrical flair and wit.

Question time is the centrepiece of parliament as theatre. It attracts the most interest from the press gallery. It has the largest audience. Australians sometimes say 'tut tut' about exchanges at question time and the level of personal abuse. There's a kids' saying that 'sticks and stones will break your bones, but names will never hurt you'. Children are notorious inventors of cruel nicknames. I still remember a kid at school called 'Dirty Jo Banana Milksop Water Gravy Moses Smith'. Another was called 'Freddy Weddy Weddy with the Little Short Legs and the Great Big Head'. Adults lapse into the habit in a less complex way. Every Crosby is called 'Bing', most Whites are called 'Snow'. Parliamentarians, some think, should be more dignified. But verbal aggression in the chamber provides a safety valve. It substitutes for the physical violence indulged in from time to time in the Japanese Diet, the Korean parliament and other legislative chambers around the world.

Others like to think of parliament as a professional debating society. There's some idealism in this view, and a touch of pomposity. The pomposity stems from the erroneous view that lots of people are listening. This is incorrect. Parliament has low ratings. The idealism comes from the notion that the parliament will be swayed by well-honed, logical and persuasive arguments. In a system dominated by political parties this is also incorrect. Politicians vote for persuasive arguments of their political opponents at their peril. The justification for parliament, either as theatre or debating society, rests on the fact that it provides a forum for the government to express its policies. More importantly, it's a forum for others to criticise the government and put alternative views. Then, as economists might say, there's a 'trickle down effect'. Some of the arguments filter through to the community. Perhaps they change people's minds.

The roles of debate and behaviour are shrouded in the history and mysteries of the Westminster system. Some of them seem silly. Others are quaint. They come from the long-established rules of the House of Commons. Speaking in the parliament, members are supposed to refer to 'the other place', rather than 'the Senate' or 'the House of Representatives'. This goes back to the days when there was such ill-feeling between the House of Commons and the House of Lords that gentlemen couldn't bring themselves to mention the name of the rival institution. In the Australian parliament I ignored this rule. I imagined a listener saying, 'What is this goose talking about?'

Another rule provides that a member of parliament who wishes to speak in the course of a division has to stand and cover his or her head, and address the chair. A book or a piece of paper is used for this purpose. This practice originated in the time when top hats were in fashion. They were removed when members entered the chamber of the House of Commons. But when members were changing their seats during a vote they put on their toppers to attract the speaker's attention. There's something a little ridiculous about standing with a piece of paper on your head. But it happens in the Australian parliament. Sometimes, in accordance with tradition, a president of the Senate or speaker of the House of Representatives will refer to himself in the third person. A Senate president in the days of the Fraser government, Sir Condor Laucke, colloquially known as 'condom', would, in moments of stress, assert his authority by standing and proclaiming, 'Order. The chair is on its feet.' It seemed an appropriate condition for a chair to be in.

These traditions, handed down from Westminster, are in reality the rules of a gentlemen's club. This is what the British parliament was in the eighteenth and nineteenth centuries. Conservative politicians, sometimes to be found on both sides of politics, think these traditions are a great idea that adds to the dignity of parliament and enhances the prestige of parliamentarians in the eyes of the community. Politics as theatre is not for them. Form counts for more than content. It's a state of mind which sits uncomfortably with an electorate intolerant of political pomposity. To contemporary Australians with aspirations for a modern democracy, these antiquated customs send strange and discordant signals.

Most of the rules relating to parliamentary language come out of the same stable. There are many forms of 'unparliamentary language'. Accusing a member of lying, dirty insinuations, using threatening language, crawling, yapping like a dog, applying Moscow rules, being a blackguard or criminally negligent are all forbidden. If these or other 'offensive' expressions are used another member may take a point of order and seek a withdrawal. If the member who has used the offensive language withdraws that is usually the end of the matter. If he or she refuses the member may be suspended. Not infrequently there is a lengthy and puerile debate as to whether the relevant words are appropriately classified as offensive. It doesn't make for good listening. At the same time complex verbal devices are used to avoid the letter of the 'lore'. Calling someone 'a liar' is offensive. Alleging 'insufficient regard for the truth' is not. The casual listener is seldom enthused by this sort of debate. They think politicians are not earning their money.

Politics is, of course, about more than theatre or debating or professional dignity. It's about policies, judgment, administration, and leadership. It's also about communication, but as the issues get more complex they become harder to explain. This is true in parliamentary democracies throughout the world. When the issues can be boiled down into simple rhetoric, the public perception of politicians improves. The Falklands War was Margaret Thatcher's greatest moment in the polls and the Gulf War a boon to political leaders in the countries which took part. Wars invoke emotional responses. The issues become relatively simple, like following a football team. The task of communicating becomes easier.

Jargon is a terrible enemy of good communication. Doctors and lawyers tend to use jargon to enhance the mystique of their profession. It gives the impression that they know exactly what they're doing, even when they don't. Since the mid 1980s, as economics has assumed a greater importance in political life, politicians have lapsed into jargon. We started to talk about J curves, fiscal drag, counter cyclical stimulation, twin deficits, structural adjustment, technical recessions and wage drift. Politicians didn't always know what they were talking about. Most people didn't know what politicians were talking about most of the time. So new kinds of judgments had to be made about taking politicians at face value, like doctors and lawyers. The guy who spoke simply and sounded like he could help you fill in your census form got the marks for communicating.

It is not surprising that there is increasing concern about 'leadership' and 'vision' in public life. Politicians sound like a bunch of chartered accountants or receivers in bankruptcy. It is not a good starting-point for spelling out a vision of the future.

It's about fifty years since George Orwell wrote his famous essay 'Politics and the English Language'. Orwell was the greatest literary advocate of plain speaking. He was not a pedant, fussed about punctuation and mixed-up tenses. But he detested euphemisms, and the manipulation of language to give a different impression from the true meaning. He objected to words like 'pacification' to describe the repressive element of British colonialism. These words were already creeping into the political language of the day. There are a lot more in the 'polspeak' of the 1990s. People accept them and distrust them at the same time. They like simplicity of expression. It is good communication.

Even highly articulate politicians lapse into comforting complexity. I heard Gareth Evans attributing Labor's 1996 defeat to 'longevity and incumbency'. Saying 'we were there too long' or 'the electorate got sick of us' might have evoked a more sympathetic response. I was stopped once by a young man in the street. 'I often think about you,' he said. 'I've heard you talking about "structural unemployment". I'm structurally unemployed and I tell you it's no different.' I stopped talking about structural unemployment.

Neville Wran and Joh Bjelke-Petersen were in totally different ways examples of politicians who at their best were successful communicators of political messages. Wran would never have made my mistake. He was, whether people liked it or not, down to earth. Joh Bjelke-Petersen was a great garbler of the language, a treasure chest of muddled ideas and mixed metaphors. He said things like, 'We don't want two bob each way. You can't sit on the fence and have one ear to the ground without dreadful things happening.' In a strange way it was usually possible to work out what he was talking about. The essential message was clear.

His wife Flo always retained a nostalgic view of the world. She recaptured in her rhetoric the simplicity of life as it used to be. Once, opening the Benalla Festival, she planted a kiss of death on me by describing me as 'a good friend'. Remonstrating with her about her kindness, I provoked a description of her visit to Benalla. She said something like this: 'It was a lovely day. There was a cavalcade of cars. I rode in an open jeep. I felt just like the Queen. People called out "Hello Flo". I thought to myself how lucky I am to be called Flo. Flo is a happy name. They like calling out "Hello Flo". It's nice to make people happy.' In the Senate I once watched as she spoke against a sales tax on shoes. 'I think of the kiddies' shoes. Their little feet grow every few months.' As she spoke she held her hands together and moved them gradually apart, like a fisherman demonstrating the size of his catch. Every parent in Australia would have understood what she was talking about. No amount of technical jargon could have countered her little demonstration.

Maybe I'm getting nostalgic too. Joh Bjelke-Petersen's most ardent supporters thought he was a man of great vision. He once advocated getting rid of all the media. 'Then,' he said, 'we would live in peace and tranquillity and no-one would know anything.' I'm sure he was right, but I don't think it's likely to happen. In the grand old days of politics, politicians didn't have the difficulty of communicating clearly on radio or television or video. The issues were much less complex. Their stage was the theatre of parliament. I suspect the actors were no better and no worse than they are today.

The Republic Debate

There is a sort of Richter Scale of feelings and emotions which people have about their own country. The French, for example, operate permanently around force eight. This is boring and irritating to others. Australians are generally much lower on the scale. For us it vacillates around particular events. The poignancy of Anzac Day, and the tradition it represents, probably arouse the most widespread emotion. Then we seem to lapse into choices we personally feel good about. I probably got up to about force eight when the Oarsome Foursome, Kieren Perkins and others climbed the dais at the Olympics in Atlanta to get their gold medals. Cathy Freeman induced similar emotions. Other happenings during the year slotted in further down the scale. Everyone has their own preference.

Jogging in London one beautiful morning in June, I came by accident upon a dress rehearsal of the Trooping of the Colour. The Horseguard Regiments and the Welsh Guards were preparing for the Queen's Birthday parade later in the month. There were marching guardsmen, mounted troopers, bands and horse-drawn carriages. Tourists from many countries, including Australia, lined the temporary barriers along Horseguard Parade. There seemed to be a general consensus that the whole performance was spectacular. And it was.

The ceremony surrounding the royal family is a big item for the British tourist industry. It's sometimes hinted that the Americans are a bit jealous about the quality of the pageantry. Tourists don't go to America to see this sort of thing. Nor do they come to Australia—although nowadays visitors fly in for

Sydney's Gay Mardi Gras. The ceremonial makes most Britons feel good. They know it's something they do better than anyone else. As an Australian of British descent watching the dress rehearsal I didn't feel anything. I thought *they* do this well. I probably would have thought the same if it had been a parade of the Canadian mounted police.

Australia's relationship with Britain has remarkable substance. It is based on history, a liberal tradition, common language and cultural aspirations, tolerance and kinship and familial ties of a large section of Australia's population. It's sufficiently strong to sustain distinct and separate allegiances across a whole range of activities.

The question of Australia becoming a republic is really a question of how people feel: the extent to which Australians feel a sense of difference from Britain about symbols and formal allegiances. There's plenty of room for debate about how a republic might be instituted. But I doubt if arguments are going to change people's feelings about whether or not we ought to have one. The arguments are too obtuse: and the lines on the chart about how people feel are fairly well drawn. If, for example, you belong to the 25 per cent or so of the Australian population born in the United Kingdom, the chances are that you will feel less sense of difference than others. You're more likely to enjoy a touch of nostalgia. If, on the other hand, you belong to the 30 per cent or so originating in continental Europe, the Middle East, Asia or South America, you probably feel no affinity with Britain at all. The chances are that you or your parents were born in a country where a cardinal principle of foreign policy was to distrust Britain. For a person like that the idea of a British monarch moonlighting as Queen of Australia seems totally inappropriate, if not offensive. It's the remainder of the population, Australians born here but of British descent, who constitute the largest pool of 'swinging voters' on this issue, and their sense of difference increases with each generation and the passing of time.

In the 1970s we adopted our own national anthem. We gave

up singing 'God Save the Queen'. It's hard to believe that it's only about twenty-five years since we stood at the start of the pictures or the football for this quaint and irrelevant song. These changes affect the strength and appropriateness of the formal connections between the two countries. They have nothing to do with the substance of the relationship.

I once sat next to a man on a long flight, a business type, with a natty briefcase. He could have been an actuary, a company director, or a brain surgeon. He asked me if I really thought Australia might become a republic. I said I didn't know, but I thought it likely at some time. He said this made him very nervous. If we became a republic, Britain or America would not come to our aid in wartime. I suggested it wouldn't make much difference either way. Britain, with the same monarch as us, had not helped us out much. The Americans hadn't come to our aid because we had a hereditary monarch. He then claimed America had helped Britain in the Falklands War because of the monarchy. This seemed a strange view.

He was, of course, an English-born Australian, entitled to a stronger sense of affinity with the royal family than most of us. But there was more sentiment than sense in his words. The idea, for example, that a titular head of state in Britain or Australia or anywhere else is going to save us in some hypothetical war is quite fanciful. It simply reinforces one of the strongest points that the republican cause has going for it. So long as Australians, of whatever ethnic origin or political persuasion, think somebody out there is going to solve our problems, the less likely we are to address them ourselves. It's the apron-string mentality. No one articulates it directly. But it still works in part of the national psyche. It implies that colonial relics have contemporary relevance.

Cardinal Newman once observed that the worst thing that could happen to a good cause is that the wrong people should embrace it. In the political climate of the 1990s politicians have been the wrong people to be embracing the republican issue. A majority of Australians are in favour of a republic but it's not a matter in the forefront of their minds. They think there are more important issues. When they do think about it, they like to think of it as something above or beyond politics. There's nothing new about this attitude. A century ago, when the colonial politicians of the day were about to establish a convention to frame the constitution, a New South Wales member of parliament put it in these terms: 'The bulk of the people at present are so busily occupied in wrestling against the adverse circumstances which have overtaken the country, they are so busy trying to earn a living, that they have very little heart and time to devote to the consideration of any question of this kind.' In spite of this the politicians grasped the nettle. They proceeded with a popularly elected convention as 'a direct call to every Australian'.

Paul Keating woke up the Rip Van Winkle of republican sentiment in 1993. He understood its symbolic power. He held it in his hand like the Welcome Stranger gold nugget. Then he dropped it in the murky waters of acrimonious partisan politics. Maybe Keating saw himself as the Houdini of Australian politics. Harry Houdini tied up his own hands and feet with seemingly unbreakable knots. He climbed into a box and had himself nailed in. Then he worked his way out of it all, and bowed to the audience. There was much applause. Keating as prime minister identified the republican debate as an issue about which Australians might develop a sense of purpose and unity. Then he tried to explain the concept: an almost impossible task in the environment of the time. His feelings on the matter seemed clearer than his thoughts. He appointed an advisory committee under the chairmanship of Malcolm Turnbull. Not surprisingly it produced a sensible report on the limited questions referred to it. But Turnbull, renowned for his combative style as much as his intelligence, couldn't build a bridge over the muddy waters of politics.

Most of the opponents of a republic in Australia agree that a republic is 'inevitable'. This is their word, not mine. They like to say it's inevitable because it makes it sound like death. And it means they don't have to do anything. They can just wait around. They think it is inevitable, because they recognise the strength and relevance of demographic and generational change. They also think it is inevitable because few people of sound mind are prepared to argue the logical alternative to inevitability: namely, that Australia would be well served by having a privileged, hereditary British monarch as head of state forever. That's hard to argue in Britain, and even harder here. So they argue that there's a hidden agenda, that the time is not yet ripe, or that the proponents of a republic have to prove that Australia would be better off. This argument is the most ludicrous of all, although superficially it is an awesome challenge. It is ludicrous because it puts the issue of the republic on the same level as a tax on petrol. It's as if the head of state is susceptible to some quantitative measure. The argument doesn't work either way. Singapore is not richer than Australia because it has a president. It's richer for a whole lot of reasons of more concern to people than the question of who is head of state.

The argument 'If it ain't broke don't fix it' has been discredited. Now people say 'Better the devil you know than the one you don't'. The devil we know is really a long line of governors-general appointed by governments of both political persuasions. Generally they have enjoyed widespread popular respect. An appointed Australian president would be no different. Others think the head of state should be as far away from Canberra as possible. Distance—even a distant monarch—lends enchantment to the view.

In his 1993 speech to the Corowa dinner marking the centenary of the conference which breathed new life into the move for an Australian federation, Paul Keating advocated a wide ranging discussion about 'the strengths and weaknesses' of Australia's constitution. This decade seems a good time to have it. It should be important to both sides of politics. Both sides should want to address the weaknesses. As Gough Whitlam pointed out in an essay on the constitution, 'the way of the reformer is hard in Australia'. That is largely because the political process is so dominated by point-scoring that it can't accommodate a debate on what might sensibly be done. That is why important issues are 'not on the agenda'. If they were they would be misrepresented. It is why any different idea gets a kicking. It's why the republic debate went off the rails. Maybe for a while politicians should devote their attention to strengthening the forums which can discuss the great issues of constitutional reform away from the pressure of day-to-day politics. That's what happened in 1893, and it worked.

A century later there are two principal republican models dithering in the wings. One provides for an Australian head of state with the same functions and powers as the governor-general, with the reserve powers spelt out and codified. The second more cautious, tentative proposal, advanced by the present prime minister, John Howard, is to hold a people's convention, to which 50 per cent of the delegates will be appointed by the government and 50 per cent elected, to explore alternatives to the first option. This is the Waiting for Something to Happen model: something less than proactive.

Opinion polls suggest that a majority of Australians favour a popularly elected president. They don't want politicians to choose a president, even if it is done by a two-thirds majority of both houses of parliament, a method which would force politicians into some necessary agreement. A president elected by a college comprising parliamentarians together with a group of directly elected citizens might provide a sensible compromise. Whatever the solution it requires an act of will by politicians, a grasping of the nettle. That's what happened a century ago.

I Have a Message from on High

Television is blamed for many things: sloppy speech, crimes of violence, promiscuity, square eyes, matrimonial disputes, radiation sickness, bad posture, lateness, poor taste, superficiality and short attention spans. I'm sure most of these things are correct. And I'm sure I've forgotten some others. Television has certainly had a dramatic effect on election campaigns.

Ben Chifley thought voters made up their minds six months before an election. But that was before elections became a media event: before TV advertising, continuous polling, direct mail, televised debates, instant images, radio talkbacks. In Chifley's day there were armies of passionate true believers lined up on each side. They turned out in thousands for political meetings in public halls. Today's politics are filtered into living rooms by television and radio. Elections are more like contests between rival management teams. The issues are narrowly focused, less sharp. Both sides seem half-pregnant with the other's policies. Personalities, credibility, images, loom larger. These days the campaign has influence. Packaged up by the media, it's right there in the living room.

The media like elections. A fortune is spent on advertising, for an unquantifiable return. Journalists, bored by the daily round of Canberra politics, have something different to write about. Some of them poke their heads out of the hothouse for a peek at the outside world. There is an avalanche of words, sometimes original, mostly recycled from something written elsewhere. Speculations are built on ghostly opinions from 'senior government sources', or 'sources close to the Liberal Party'. Headlines tantalise with conflicting images. In 1996 they were 'Keating lashes Howard', 'Fight to the Death', 'Howard savages Keating': newspapers keeping up with TV. Thoughtful analysis falls victim to deadlines. So, when I asked a senior Canberra journalist in February 1996 what he thought about the election, he replied, 'I'm not sure. But I've been on holidays. I feel terrific. At the end of a couple of weeks I'll be ratshit.'

Television stations produce a daily round-up of the campaign. They assemble expert panels, which award points for this and that, like judges at a dog show. 'Sleeper' issues are discovered. Meters measure performances in debates. About three weeks into a campaign someone discovers that the real issues aren't being dealt with. Predictions are made about outcomes, in particular states, or particular marginal seats. They're mostly guesses. And often wrong. Campaign television images are different. Political leaders drive their wagons into marginal seats. They are seen in shopping malls, at farm gates, in pubs. The backgrounds look normal, except for the ubiquitous staffer in the Hugo Boss suit, pacing in circles, talking into a mobile phone.

Between elections Canberra is the focus of federal politics. During an election it reverts to its natural state, a tranquil lawn-cemetery of national aspiration. The politicians are all out of town, active at the rim rather than the hub. The bureaucracy relaxes and waits. Old briefings are pulled out, and polished up, ready for new ministers in whichever government takes office.

There is a big gap between those involved in the feverish activity of an election campaign and the general public. The pulse rates are points apart. Politicians unfairly get all the blame for all the hype. The polls tell us that most people don't believe politicians. Scepticism is deep-seated. Perhaps it's nothing new. Certainly, a healthy Australian irreverence has been round for a long time. In 1977 I campaigned for the Labor candidate, Ritchie Gunn, in the South Australian seat of Kingston. A doctor and talented musician, he had a jazz band called 'Ritchie Gunn and his Hot Six'. As an innovation, we campaigned in shopping malls, travelling in a van from one centre to the next. At each stop the band played. It was good stuff, and a crowd quickly gathered. Between brackets Ritchie Gunn and I spruiked political messages through a microphone. When the music stopped the crowd drifted away, as people took kids to the toilet, picked up the vegies, collected a trolley for the groceries. When the music started again they came back. Politics seemed like a tough game. Normal priorities and election campaigns didn't seem to mix.

The Ritchie Gunn innovation was a step back towards old-style campaigning. It was face-to-face. You could see that people were more interested in jazz than politics. You had a feel for your audience as they melted away. Old-style electioneering was a participatory experience, genuinely interactive. Watching politics on television is a 'what you see is what you get' experience. He or she talks at you. You can hiss, boo, clap, interject at your set, but there's no reaction. Devices like studio audiences and talkback radio are an attempt at participation. To assemble a studio audience, TV stations round up the usual suspects. Mostly they're single-issue people, zealots having a night out. There's a moderator who moulds the debate according to his own sense of the superficial. Talkback radio has its own set of junkies, often planted by the political parties. Most talkback hosts are overbearing, intruding their own vacuous opinions. Callers are interrupted, cut off, sent packing. Time is important: an advertising break is coming up. It's about the best the electronic media can do.

Dr William Maloney, the Labor member for the federal seat of Melbourne from 1904 to 1940, used to do his election campaigning on street corners. The meetings would be advertised by someone walking through the streets ringing a bell, like a town crier. The time and place of the meeting would be called out. Everyone in the neighbourhood knew it was on. Anyone could turn up: to applaud, catcall, shake hands, ask questions. Everyone knew Maloney, and he remained in parliament a long time. Jim Cairns, as a new candidate for parliament, did the same thing as late as 1955. Television arrived a year later.

The nice thing about old-style campaigning was that political leaders had to get out and meet people, and people had a real chance to meet politicians. There was no electronic curtain between the voter and the candidate. Curtin, Chifley and Menzies travelled round the country addressing meetings in town halls and city squares. The faithful and sometimes the heretics would gather in large numbers. There'd be arguments, scuffles, applause and disruption. Mostly people had a good time. In the 1960s things changed. Political leaders' meetings became carefully staged media events, directed less at real people than the euphemistic 'wider audience'. The participatory election meeting fell into decline. Politicians became less real.

The fact that modern election campaigns turn largely on the daily utterances of the leaders, reported on nightly television, doesn't prevent a bit of the old stuff going on, particularly in marginal electorates. Party bureaucrats attempt to use all available resources to try and win votes. Sometimes it's futile activity, at worst counterproductive. Ministers and shadow ministers are dispatched all over the place to doorknock, spruik, fundraise and encourage the faithful. A lot of energy goes up the spout. In the year of 'Ritchie Gunn and his Hot Six' I kept a campaign diary. The Labor Party was in opposition, led by Gough Whitlam. Malcolm Fraser was trying to win a second term as prime minister. A few entries are a reminder of things past:

Tuesday, Canberra. The parliamentary session finished today with the normal flurry of 'urgent' legislation crammed through in a few minutes. We have been here for weeks padding out debates on trivial issues. Today nothing is more important than getting the parliament wound up. The blood has been rushing to many heads. We will go home tomorrow then off on the campaign trail.

Tuesday, a week later, Tasmania. Took late afternoon flight to Launceston to speak at a fundraising barbecue for the ALP candidate. Tasmania exudes an air of extraordinary calm. Suspect nobody has told them about the election.

The barbecue was in a native bush park, above the Tamar River on the outskirts of the city. Might have been pleasant but for the temperature—probably below freezing point—and a strong, gusty wind. A small crowd of ALP supporters huddled round the fireplaces trying to cook sausages and chops and warm their hands. I worried if older ones would survive the evening and be able to vote. At about 9 p.m. I climbed up on the edge of a stone barbecue fireplace and, with flames licking my feet, gave a November 11 memorial oration from the middle of a cloud of smoke. Felt I must look like Joan of Arc or Hamlet's ghost. Tried to capture inspirational message of both: keep the visions and revenge the foul doings of the past. Had to stop when my feet became too hot. The audience clapped their frozen hands: a muffled sound of gloves. They rushed for their cars. Later I was taken to a fundraising 'sing-along' at a school for deaf children. The audience there seemed warmer and enthusiastic. An unambiguous and worthwhile cause: no grey areas like politics.

Three days later, Melbourne. The last three days have been spent rushing round Melbourne speaking at schools, doing radio broadcasts and trying to put some speech notes together for various audiences. The shape of events is already beginning to change each day. It is a struggle to keep up with the key issues. Yesterday I agreed to do some doorknocking for the candidate in a bayside electorate. I was given a small street map of 'my area' and trudged up a long, hot hill beside a park before coming to the first house. I knocked and waited for a while before the door was opened by a little old lady. I gave her the standard spiel, but she seemed unconvinced and told me she intended to vote for the government. I politely inquired why. 'If you must know young man,' she said, pointing upwards with her index finger and smiling sweetly, 'I have a message from on high.' Very disconcerting. They have more funds and Him as well.

Next day, Sydney. Here for the policy speech in the Opera House. Told to be there early and be seated in front row. Going into the Opera House I ran into George Negus. He complained that an old lady had hit him with her umbrella for being nasty to me on his program the night before.

The auditorium was full—an audience of fairly subdued party stalwarts applauding appropriately. Lots of glitz. 'Warm-up' speeches and then the policy speech. There were a few promises which most of us in the front row hadn't heard of before. Some people scratched their heads—Bob Hawke indulged himself with a couple of undiluted expletives. It was all too late, however. We were under way.

Three days later, Adelaide. Started the day with a press conference. Half a dozen journalists turned up and I talked about policy issues. At lunch time, I went out to a whitegoods factory to speak to the workers during their lunch hour. The meeting took place on a scruffy lawn, dotted with privet hedges, in front of an ugly brick building. It was boiling hot. The public address system cracked like an electric storm. The 'workers' huddled in groups in the shade of the privet hedges. I stood out in the sun and talked while they ate their pies and drank coke. I had the feeling that they were rather sorry for me. This I understood. I spoke about unemployment. When I finished, the chairman asked if there were any questions. There was a long pause. Then a man with glassy eyes slowly got up from under a privet bush. 'I'm very worried about Uray ne um,' he announced. 'What are you going to do about Uray ne um?' I told him we were more against it than the others and he seemed pleased. No more questions. Afterwards, I shook hands with some of the audience and then they strolled slowly back to work. Glassy eyes remained behind to talk about Uray ne um. I asked him what his job was. He said he did odd jobs. I said that didn't sound the best job to have. 'I like it,' he replied. 'I've been ten years in a mental institution and after that any job is pretty good.' I wondered why I'd chosen to talk about unemployment.

Next day, Melbourne. This morning I received a telegram from the party's national campaign committee advising that the opinion polls showed that we had a small lead over the government. Surveys indicated unemployment as being the main issue with a majority of the electorate. We are urged to concentrate on this issue. Unfortunately the day's news indicates a degree of confusion in relation to our policy on taxation. The shadow treasurer was interviewed in Cairns and said that, if there were any need to clear anything up, it would be done next Friday. One wonders what we're supposed to say in the meantime.

Next day, Adelaide. Campaigned today in a suburban

electorate after a series of poorly attended meetings with 'interest' groups. Should be called 'not interested' groups. In the afternoon I was scheduled to speak to sixty students of journalism at a college of advanced education. As a result of some organisational stuff-up, they weren't there. I ended up listening to their tedious lecturer giving me the benefit of his views. Later I was supposed to meet some people in a pub, but they weren't there either. I finished the day having a counter tea with the candidate. Not a productive day.

Next day, Melbourne. This afternoon, I spoke at a well-organised and well-attended policy seminar to which the three major parties (Liberal, Labor and Democrats) were invited. To the embarrassment of a section of the audience, nobody turned up from the Liberal Party. Don Chipp seemed to agree with most of the things I said, but emphasised his greater interest in 'freedom', 'goodness' and 'decency'. He seemed worried about DLP attacks on his party. 'They're spreading the story that I didn't get in the Fraser cabinet because I stuff animals,' he whispered.

'Is that true, Don?' I asked.

'You bastard,' he said, with his infectious grin. He's hard to dislike . . . something he's got going for him in this election.

At the end of the seminar, an anxious young man operating the tape recorder informed me that the tape had picked up the whispered conversation between Chipp and myself. Did I want it erased? 'No,' I said, 'there ought to be an accurate record of the occasion.'

Next day, Sydney. At Sydney airport, it was already hot at 10 a.m. I was picked up and driven to a large meatworks on the far outskirts of the city. We arrived at noon. Opposite the huge, grey, sprawling meatworks, a little old man in a Panama hat was standing in the hot sun in the centre of a large flat paddock. He held a banner saying 'ALP Meeting'. There was no-one in sight except for a bloke with a gladstone bag, sitting under a distant gum tree eating his lunch. I asked nervously when the audience was expected to arrive. 'Better give them five minutes,' said the old man apologetically. We waited ten minutes, and no-one appeared. Then a car came across the paddock. The driver said he was the union rep. from the meatworks. 'Sorry about this,' he said, 'real balls-up . . . we've got problems. We've been having political meetings in the canteen for thirty years and just yesterday the management said you couldn't come into the plant. The troops were pretty pissed off, so I called a mass meeting at eight o'clock this morning. They all turned up. I moved a motion that we stop work at twelve o'clock, walk out of the works and have the meeting here in the paddock.'

'Well where are they?' I asked.

'You wouldn't believe it,' he said, 'but some bastard moved an amendment that we stop work straight away and go home. It was carried. Everyone's gone home. I think we better go over to the bowling club and have a drink. There will be some meatworkers over there.'

At the bowling club I went up to the bar to buy some drinks. 'How's things,' I said to a young man propped against the bar.

'Shithouse, mate—can't earn a quid. I work at the meatworks. The bloody union is always on strike. No future in it.' He asked me my name. I told him. 'Jesus, mate,' he said, 'you've started another one.'

Next stop was a civic reception in Baulkham Hills, a nearby shire—Liberal territory. On the way, the candidate pointed out a rather opulent new housing subdivision. 'There's a big swing to us in there,' he said—the psyched-up euphoria which grabs all political candidates.

The reception took place in a room resembling a funeral parlour and attended by councillors and a number of large small-businessmen. Plenty of scotch and sandwiches. The president said that the shire might be considered affluent, but it had many problems which seemed to be ignored in Canberra. Would a Labor government remember Baulkham Hills? I mopped the sweat from my forehead. I had already decided that I'd never forget Baulkham Hills. But in replying I made no promises. I spoke of the crisis in all levels of government in Australia. The councillors nodded wisely.

Next day, Tasmania. I flew to the north west coast of Tasmania this morning. I was met at the airport by a 'salt of the earth' ALP lady who drove me to the first meeting. In the car she chatted away about the election . . . full of intelligent and perceptive observations about how it was all going at the 'grass roots' level. She works hard for the party, writes a column in the local paper and probably organises half the 'happenings' in the town where she lives . . . one of those who deserves better from parliamentarians and the political system.

We were supposed to meet the candidate at a particular venue, but he didn't arrive and sent his wife instead. During the day I had a number of desultory meetings, cups of tea, and lunch with various party stalwarts, but I don't think I met anyone who was not either a member of the party or a committed supporter.

Next day, Melbourne. This evening Bob Hawke and I spoke at a meeting in a primary school hall. We had dinner first in a new, cavernous and gloomy hotel-motel . . . colonial baroque architecture and plastic food.

There was not a very big crowd at the meeting. Bob Hawke kept muttering, 'There's something wrong.' I think he meant he was used to bigger audiences.

Next day, Melbourne. This morning I campaigned in an outer suburban electorate which should swing back to Labor.

As instructed, I arrived at a large shopping centre at 10 a.m. There was to be a march against unemployment from one shopping centre to the next. I was to speak at each centre. There was a small collection of party activists armed with lurid banners to meet me. After I had spoken, we formed into line and marched off down the main street with banners aloft. It all reminded me sadly of Dad's Army. Our main achievement was to cause a traffic jam and a number of resentful and irate motorists. At the second shopping centre, it was basically the same audience, so I gave a different speech. As the meeting broke up, a cavalcade of brightly decorated cars with Democrat slogans swept into the car park . . . Don Chipp in front, standing up in an open car, like the Queen reviewing the Horse Guards. There were more irate motorists and more hooting of horns.

Two days later, Melbourne. I have addressed five or six meetings in the last four days at factories in outer suburban electorates. The procedures are nearly always the same . . . a public address system is set up, you wait for the workers to trickle out, and then they receive the doubtful benefit of a few speeches. Occasionally, they ask a few questions. At one meeting, the audience consisted almost entirely of Turkish women. I don't think many of them understood anything I said. The discussion after these meetings has been interesting and depressing. There is a lot of criticism of trade unions and a widespread acceptance of the view that unemployment is caused by high wages. When you ask them about this, it is apparent that it is never their wages which are too high, but rather the bloke next door. There is also anxiety about jobs, but they blame many factors for this, not just the government. Somehow, during these discussions, I realised that we have no hope in this election.

Last day, Melbourne. Polling day for a politician is something like Christmas Eve for a child. You spend it in hope, performing a number of politically necessary but probably futile tasks and just wait and wait until 10 p.m. when you begin to have a clear idea what has happened. There were no goodies for us this time. We watched Gough Whitlam concede defeat with dignity. Then to bed. Perhaps the bruises will heal over the long hot summer.

That's the way it used to be. I suppose it's what people mean when they talk about 'the democratic process'. It's always been informed by a strong dose of scepticism, sometimes healthy, sometimes not. Politicians hover between euphoria and despair. The electorate probably feels the same. In an election campaign they exchange 'vibes'.

Plenty of ill-informed and sometimes silly people get to vote at elections. But mostly voters make thoughtful and understandable decisions. In spite of all the talk, the analysis, the advertising, they suspect that whoever wins an election the national debt will not disappear overnight, unemployment will not suddenly become a thing of the past, the football season will start at the end of March, the price of cars and houses will remain about the same. Retailers will complain. The Australian team will go to the Olympics. Births, deaths and marriages will appear each day in the papers. And for another three years politics will go back to Canberra, followed by those who want to follow it, and ignored by those who don't. And for most people life will go on as usual in this not too unpleasant land. And during the election campaign they'll be like that lot in the Adelaide shopping mall. They'll take the kids to the toilet, pick up the vegies, load up the groceries. If they like what they hear, they will stop for a while and listen to the music—but not, perhaps, for very long.

Postcards

I Traveel All Zee Time

NOT LONG ago on a flight to Japan I sat next to a plump, stocky man with a squarish head. He had a short haircut and a clipped little moustache, like Hitler's. We began to talk over lunch. 'Zee beef ees good,' he said, before inquiring politely why I'd chosen the Japanese meal instead. 'I traveel all zee time,' he said, 'but I cannot eat zee Japon food.' He told me he worked for the International Olive Oil Council.

'I've met plenty of snake oil salesmen,' I said, 'but you're the first olive oil salesman I've ever met.'

He looked slightly miffed. 'I am not,' he said, 'a salesman. I am a diplomat.'

This, I thought, can't be right: a diplomat from the Kingdom of Olive Oil? 'Perhaps,' I suggested, 'you're more of a missionary promoting the virtues of olive oil.'

He didn't seem to understand the word 'missionary'. 'I'm diplomat,' he insisted, 'I traveel to many countries. Australia. Eet is no probleme. Thees year you haf planted 600,000 olive trees in Australia. It ees very good. Japan and other countries ees not so good. Japan peeple and Asia peeple no like zee olive oil. I travel to promote zee Mediterranean gastronomique. It ees difficult but in Australia it ees good.'

I found this interesting. My previous ignorance of the olive oil business had been profound. We shook hands at the airport. He gave me his card. 'I'll remember you when I see a bottle of olive oil,' I said.

'No! No! No!' he replied. 'Remember me when you eet it.'

I suspect that experienced airline travellers develop techniques for dealing with fellow passengers—particularly the one you happen to be sitting next to. It's an unusual situation being a fellow prisoner jointly constrained in an enforced intimacy for anything up to ten hours. Then the plane lands at some alien airport and you each escape to pursue resumed lives and different destinations. In the meantime there is no way out, no walking away, no changing your mind.

I've developed a particular routine, which has the force of habit. I sit down, say 'good morning' or 'good afternoon' to the person in the next seat, and start straight into a book or a newspaper. Morning tea or the first meal is the time for some exploratory chitchat. Then you're locked into your airline highchair and confronted by a cluttered tray. Reading a book becomes difficult; reading a newspaper impossible. A meal is convivial. And by that time the body language from the next seat has probably told you something about your travelling companion.

There seem to be certain conversational rules embracing safe topics, beginning with the airline food, whether you are travelling on holiday or business, the meals of various airlines, comparative experiences of flying. Once I developed an unusual relationship with a young South American woman without any conversation at all. Flying into Hong Kong through a cyclonic storm the aircraft began to shudder, pitching and tossing like a small boat in a raging sea. Outside the clouds were black and swirling. Suddenly the young woman had hold of my left hand, squeezing it with the grip of her Amazon ancestors. I squeezed back, temporarily enjoying the feeling of being of some use. I tried to reassure her. I pretended to read my book, as if the whole thing was a completely normal experience. But fear can be transmitted through the fingertips. Before long I was as anxious as she was and grateful for her firm grip. At Hong Kong airport she looked white and shaken. I imagine I looked the same. Most of the passengers did. A Japanese gentleman across the aisle stepped over and shook my hand. 'Congratulashions,' he said. He seemed to have started a fashion. The passengers were all shaking hands with each other like communicants at the end of a Mass. I shook hands with the South American woman. 'Muchas gracias,' she said.

'And thank you too,' I replied.

Looking at all those jumbos taking off from busy airports like Singapore and Hong Kong, you wonder how many passengers are in the air at any one time. I imagine hundreds of thousands: people leaving old jobs or travelling to new ones, tourists, pilgrims, business people, soldiers, olive oil diplomats. The list must be endless. Mostly they're preoccupied with jet lag, sleeping and eating, a film, possible turbulence, the challenges awaiting them at their destination. Not many can expect to find romance on an aircraft, the way people once did on ships. I've discovered, however, that there are some who do, and apparently succeed.

I can't, for example, persuade a Sydney acquaintance of mine to tell me much about his frequent visits overseas. I know he's a businessman, and I know he works hard. But to find out what he actually does or thinks about in any of the countries he visits is beyond me. 'How was America?' I once asked him.

'It was OK,' he said. 'I stopped in Hawaii on the way back. But listen to this. When I boarded the plane for Sydney, I found myself sitting next to this unbelievably gorgeous woman: long blonde hair, fantastic legs and a really beautiful face. She was, I assure you, all woman. It turned out to be an extraordinary flight.'

'That's all very well,' I said, bereft of similar gossip or competing enthusiasm. 'She was probably a painfully boring, dumb blonde.'

'Don't you believe it,' he said. 'She is one of the most interesting people I've ever talked to. She certainly isn't dumb. She has a PhD in anthropology from Cornell University.'

'Go on,' I said. 'How old is she, 110?'

He gave me a patronising smile. 'She looks about twenty-eight. In fact, she's thirty-six. And divorced,' he added, in a tone suggesting another special attribute. 'One of those people who's been around a bit,' he went on, 'but remains a very warm person.'

'Well,' I asked, 'what happened?'

He looked at me reproachfully, as if I'd trampled on a flower bed of delicate emotions. 'I said goodbye to her at Sydney airport. That wasn't easy. She was going straight on to Brisbane. But would you believe it? She's coming back to Sydney for five days in a month's time. And it happens to be in the week that my wife is going to visit her parents in Perth. Can you believe that?'

'Of course I believe it,' I said. 'You've always been lucky.' What else could I say? He seemed genuinely besotted.

It was probably two months before I saw him again. My curiosity still had the better of me. Over a coffee I managed to ask, in an offhand way, 'Incidentally, how did that business with the American woman work out?'

'What American woman?' he said.

'You know,' I blurted out, 'the one with the blonde hair and good legs, the beautiful anthropologist from Cornell.'

He poked at his cappuccino with a teaspoon, creating a hole like a miniature volcano in the froth. For what seemed like a minute he gazed pensively into the volcano as if he was trying to recall something. 'Oh, yes,' he said. 'The week she was in Sydney I had to go to Bangkok. So I missed her.'

'I suppose that's the way it goes,' I said sympathetically. I was about to ask, 'How's Bangkok these days?' but I wasn't quick enough.

'I had this extraordinary flight home,' he said. 'I found myself sitting next to this gorgeous woman . . . she was incredible . . . fine boned, petite, big eyes, a bit like Audrey Hepburn. She was half Thai, half French. It has to be one of the most appealing mixtures you could find anywhere. We seemed to relate to each other from the time the flight attendant served the first drink . . . the one before take-off. Interestingly enough she told me she really liked Australian men—well, intelligent, sensitive ones,' he added with a self-deprecating smile.

'Oh, yeah,' I said gruffly, 'what did you talk about? I suppose you told her how intelligent and sensitive you were.'

'As a matter of fact,' he said, 'we talked mainly about her. She's had an interesting life. Brought up in Paris and Bangkok, educated at the Sorbonne, worked for UNESCO, a failed marriage. In fact her divorce had just come through. She seemed a bit sad about it. She put her head on my shoulder, we had a few drinks and just talked quietly all night. I've never known the time pass so quickly on an overnight flight from Bangkok.'

'She sounds interesting,' I said. 'How old was she? I suppose you were cradle-snatching again.'

'Not at all,' he said, 'she was thirty-six.' His eyes drifted away from the volcano in the coffee cup, and into the middle distance.

Thinking back over these and similar conversations with this guy, it's easy to conclude that he's got problems. Anyone could have a go at diagnosing them. But he's also intelligent, well educated and charming. Maybe he travels too much. Perhaps all his flights are like romantic shipboard cruises to the Caribbean. I'm sure he sits next to interesting women on aeroplanes. But they can't all be thirty-six. Surely they can't all be divorced? There's a bit of fantasy in it all, rounded out to suit his sense of appropriateness. And the possibilities seem unfulfilled, thwarted by airline seats and airport partings. He can't quite get hold of them. Touches of the leisured lifestyle, they elude him like elegant smoke rings from a Cuban cigar.

One thing is for sure. He likes telling me about his experiences. He watches my face as he talks. He wants to make sure I've savoured every delicious and intimate moment. It's as if he's saying, 'You spend a bit of time on aeroplanes too. But I bet you've never had an experience like this one.' I find this a bit frustrating. I can't have a conversation with him, comparing notes as it were. I've sat next to lots of people on aeroplanes, but the truth is I've never had an experience to compare with his. I've rummaged through my memory trying to find something with a touch of sensual excitement about it, something a bit out of the ordinary. There is nothing to be found, at least nothing I can compare notes about.

I caught my first aeroplane when I was eleven: Melbourne to Sydney. I was going for a week's holiday in Sydney with an aunt and uncle. My aunt had no children of her own, and was generous with nephews and nieces. She paid the fare. My mum drove me down from Ballarat to Essendon Airport. She told me to be very careful in Sydney: it was a much more wicked place than Ballarat.

'Don't worry Mum,' I said, 'nothing will happen to me.' On the plane the TAA hostesses were very kind. They gave me a seat next to the window, with a spare seat next to me and some magazines to read. It seemed like a great adventure. After about an hour a man came and sat in the seat next to me. He was, I guessed, about fifty-five with a florid smiling face and thick grey hair in a sort of bouffant style. He asked me my name, and where I went to school, and what I was going to do in Sydney, and whether someone was meeting me at the airport. I told him my name and my school. I said I was visiting my aunt in Sydney. He said he thought we could be friends. He was a businessman with a big house in Sydney. Perhaps I could come and visit him? I said I'd have to discuss that with my aunt. As we talked I turned over the pages of *Walkabout* magazine which I had on my lap. There were two pages of pictures of bare-breasted African women standing on a beach. In those days the photos were a bit risqué.

The man looked down at the pictures. 'How does that affect you?' he asked.

'They're Africans,' I replied, 'African women on a beach.'

He gave me an effusive smile. 'If I slipped my hand under the magazine could I feel it?' he said.

'Feel what?' I squeaked, but too late. His hand was already there fumbling with the buttons on my trousers. I wondered if this was what people did on aeroplanes. I desperately wanted to ask my mum.

Then a voice said, 'Would you mind moving back to your seat now, sir.' It was a hostess who'd been walking up and down the aisle. The man got up and, without a word, returned to his seat. The hostess came and sat beside me. 'I'll sit here for a while,' she said, 'and we'll have a chat. Do you know that man who was sitting next to you?'

'No.'

'OK,' she said, 'I wouldn't talk to him again. Just forget it.' She was very kind and it seemed quite romantic sitting next to her in her uniform. Sadly I can't really remember what she looked like. With hindsight I'm prepared to believe she had a beautiful face, long blonde hair and terrific legs. Maybe she was thirty-six and divorced. To me it never mattered what she looked like. I just remember her as a gorgeous woman.

At Sydney airport I walked quickly across the tarmac and into the terminal. As I pushed through the crowd I heard a man's voice behind me. 'John, John,' it said, 'come with me for a minute. There's something I want to show you.'

I remembered what the hostess had said. I began to run towards the place where my aunt had told me to meet her. Fortunately she was there waiting. 'What on earth is the matter?' she said. 'Didn't you like the aeroplane?'

'It was OK.'

'Who was that man calling out to you?'

'Just another passenger,' I said breathlessly. My aunt and I got into a taxi and drove into Sydney. I didn't tell her much about the plane trip. And when I got home from my holiday I didn't tell my mum and dad either. I suspected I'd never be allowed to go to Sydney again. When I got much older I still didn't tell anyone. I thought I might finish up on a Derryn Hinch or Ray Martin program.

Needless to say I couldn't bring myself to tell my experienced traveller friend about this story. It all happened so long ago. It's lacking in romance. Though I remember the man vividly I can't remember the gorgeous woman. I lack the power of imagination to turn it into a story as fantastic as his experiences. I'm grateful to have met dozens of interesting people, sitting in the next seat on aeroplanes. Next time I meet my traveller friend it could well be for a lunch. I'll tell him about the olive oil man as I eat my salad. My friend will tell me about his latest airborne romance. That's the way it goes.

Flying into the Future

On a long flight I feel happier if the person sitting next to me seems comfortable and relaxed—a normal sort of person doing normal things, like eating or reading or watching a movie. Strange, twitchy people make me feel ill at ease. If a man sitting next to me twitches a lot, I start to wonder if he might be an amateur hijacker: the sort of bloke who'd do a botched job.

On one occasion, flying to Hong Kong, I had a Chinese guy sitting next to me. He had a wild-looking head of curly hair, a round plump face, thick lips, and spectacles with very thick lenses. I tried to read the newspapers. He sat staring intently at the small video screen a couple of feet in front of his face. He ate his meal as if in a trance, never taking his eyes off the screen. I couldn't help noticing that the screen was blank. He kept on staring at it, without moving a muscle. I began to get twitchy and ill at ease. Finally it all got the better of me. I touched him on the arm and said inquiringly 'No pictures?'

He turned the thick lenses in my direction like an irritated robot. 'It is,' he said, 'owt ohf ohda,' and turned back to the screen.

I went back to my newspaper, but I couldn't concentrate. Perhaps, I thought, he can see something with those thick lenses which I can't see. Perhaps he was thinking about the phenomenon of failed technology, or a world without television. I was still wondering about it when we landed at Hong Kong.

In some ways Hong Kong is like my travelling companion's video screen. It's hard to get a clear picture of the place. It's remembered by most as a series of experiences, recorded as snapshots in the mind: a floating restaurant, a romance, a ferry ride, a business deal. One clear thing, however, is that it's not out of order. It looks as if it's in the hands of a frenetic child prodigy, with a giant Lego set. Block after block of high-rise apartments are arranged in geometric huddles on every available patch of land. Low-rise buildings are tumbled over to be replaced by bigger ones. In the harbour, hundreds of floating cranes are bunched together like fiddlesticks in a hand which points them skywards. The commercial spires of the world's multinationals and luxury hotels jostle each other on the skyline. Even a cemetery climbs up the side of a hill to the top, the gravestones arranged in neat but crowded rows.

Hong Kong becomes part of China in 1997. In 1984 the British and the Chinese negotiated an artful formula for the transition, known as the 'One Country, Two Systems' agreement. The country will be China, and the systems socialism on the mainland and capitalism in Hong Kong. The agreement is supposed to run for fifty years. There is some political uncertainty in Hong Kong about all of this. A significant group of Hong Kong's Chinese community is apprehensive about China's intentions. But they seem to be coping with it. As they do with the management of six million people in a tiny area of land. You don't get the sense that things are out of order. The public transport works. The port works. People have jobs.

It all works because Hong Kong seems to know what it's about. What it is about is continuing to be the main gateway to China, the world's largest market, bigger than Europe, North America, Japan and Indonesia combined. So, for an estimated cost of twenty-two billion Australian dollars, Hong Kong is building a huge new airport on an island, reclaiming land, and continually upgrading the port. From the air you can see the towers of the new suspension bridge which will connect the airport with Hong Kong island. It will be longer than the Golden Gate Bridge in San Francisco. The administration has announced the planned building of a massive new convention centre on an island which will itself be artificially built. The hands of the Lego set fanatic are working overtime.

Australians have not been left flat-footed in racing after business opportunities. An estimated 20,000 Australians live in Hong Kong. The Australian Hong Kong Chamber of Commerce boasts about 1500 members. I remember it in days gone by as a handful of disgruntled refugees from the Australian taxation system. Trade between Australia and Hong Kong is booming along. A very British, but Chinese, gentleman complained to me that the Australian business presence is disproportionately large. Close to 1000 Australian companies now have operations in mainland China. The gateway is all hustle and bustle.

In a good year Hong Kong has nine million visitors. Its tourist industry is alive and well, catered for, in part, by eighty first-class hotels which, with one or two exceptions, resemble lavishly sculptured filing cabinets, but are distinguished by their quality of service. As a guest you're made to feel that they've been waiting anxiously for you to arrive.

I can't imagine that nine million visitors go to Hong Kong to enjoy the 'Pearly Gates' feeling in the foyer of a well-run hotel. They go, of course, for business reasons, to browse and shop, and perhaps pick up a bit of the latest electronic gadgetry with which Hong Kong Chinese are obsessed. Perhaps some go to catch a comfortable glimpse of the future, because Hong

Kong is also the gateway to a different sort of world, a world where the old order changes, yielding its place to the new. And some must go to Hong Kong because physically it still retains a touch of magic. It's a magic which comes from a backdrop of craggy mountains, and because this is a city which embraces the sea. The harbour bustles with life and commerce, lights twinkle and reflect in the water. Sydney has some of the same magic, and so does Hobart in a rustic way. Melbourne, which turned its back on the water, does not. In Hong Kong, if you can open the curtains and watch the harbour, it doesn't much matter if the TV is out of order.

At Hong Kong airport I waited in a departure queue thirty metres long. A man behind me tapped me on the shoulder. He was an Australian I'd known some years ago. Now he's working for a media company with world-wide television interests. He spends, he told me, most of his life on aeroplanes, and was heading for Los Angeles. He talked like a series of ten-second TV grabs strung together. 'Executives,' he said, 'do it tough.' 'You don't grow fat on airline food.' 'Los Angeles was,' he told me, 'death row,' Britain 'a cultural artefact,' and Hong Kong 'the future.' His eyes glazed over slightly. He began to talk about markets, markets for television, millions of viewers. Hong Kong was the gateway to it all.

As we said goodbye he seemed suddenly to remember we both came from Australia. 'How's your football team going?' he asked. I told him the dismal truth. 'It's a bit like life, isn't it,' he said. 'It's how you finish which counts.' Another TV grab for me to think about on the next flight. I did. I imagined him on yet another aeroplane flying into Hong Kong's new airport, and gazing intently into a vacant video screen. Like his boss, he'd be 'very focused'. He'd be flying into the future, dreaming about millions of TV sets. It wouldn't matter much if his was out of order.

The House of Dr Sun Yat Sen

There was a handsome brochure on the writing desk in my hotel room. It was well designed and nicely printed, like the brochures in all the rooms in all the big international hotel chains. The brochure was called 'What to do in Shanghai'. It recommended a visit to the Bund, a river cruise, antique shops, the Pearl Tower (the tallest in Asia), the Peace Hotel, things like that. Things suitable for a western visitor to do.

The entry which caught my eye was one headed 'The House of Dr Sun Yat Sen'. It said that the former residence of Sun Yat Sen, the founder of modern China, was located in the old French concession, close to the hotel. It contained antiques and memorabilia from the late nineteenth and the early twentieth century. In 1924 Sun Yat Sen had negotiated terms for co-operation with the fledgling Chinese Communist Party in the very same house. 'Once inside you really feel you've stepped back into the 1920s.' Guests should inquire at the concierge desk for directions.

I had an hour or so to spare. Stepping back into the 1920s seemed like a nice idea. At the concierge desk there were three young men dressed in pageboy outfits, like extras in a New York musical. 'I want,' I said, 'to go to the house of Dr Sun Yat Sen.'

One of them peered over the counter, looking me up and down. 'I think,' he said, 'you should go to the hospital.'

'No, no,' I protested, 'I don't want to go to the hospital. I want,' I repeated slowly, 'to go to the house of Dr Sun Yat Sen. Do you know who he is?'

He looked at me with a blank stare. 'I know who he is,' said one of his colleagues. 'He is a good doctor. But Dr Wei Feng is better.' He started to write Dr Wei Feng's address on a piece of paper.

I said not to bother. 'I'm feeling much better.'

I had to abandon my trip back to the 1920s. The delegation I was with had an official program: a meeting with the vice-mayor, a day in the Pudong industrial zone, a visit to the new stock exchange, a seminar with Chinese businessmen, and discussions with government officials. It was all about contemporary China: lots of men in grey suits with briefcases.

There is a sense in which the history and image of Shanghai is a creation of the western imagination. Chinese history, as the Chinese understand it, is as ancient as Old King Cole. A century disappears in aeons of time, like a ship in the Bermuda Triangle. In this culture Shanghai is not an old city. In the early nineteenth century it was a village on a turbid river, but a few kilometres from the mouth of the Yangtze, one of the great trade waterways into the interior of China. The modern city of Shanghai, like Australia, was invented by the British. They needed a new trading port, particularly for the ships bringing opium from India. Shanghai was well situated for this purpose. The Chinese didn't like this idea. So in 1839 the British declared war, quickly defeating the Chinese, and establishing the so-called British concession. There they built a consulate and the palatial residences of British merchants. It was a time when the names of opium merchants like Matheson and Jardine, or the Americans Beale and Dent, first appeared in the chronology of western involvement in China. The Americans carved out a concession for themselves. So did the French. On the Bund, a fine boulevard facing the Whangpoo River, the Europeans built great Victorian palaces of commerce. The Bund and the concessions were western enclaves. Few Chinese were admitted.

Until 1949 Shanghai provided most of its large western community with a lifestyle upon which Scott Fitzgerald might have cast a benign eye. The Japanese occupation interrupted, but it was only an interruption. Fortunes were made. Clubs were the centres of social life. Corruption and vice seemed endemic. The city had British, American, white Russian, French and Jewish communities. It seemed cosmopolitan. But the bits remained aloof from each other. And from the Chinese.

Today's Shanghai has a population of fourteen million people. In the evening the Bund is crowded with Chinese out for a stroll. Cranes dominate the skyline. The streets thump with the sound of jackhammers. Across the river the huge industrial estate of Pudong rises out of the mud flats. The Pearl Tower, ostensibly for telecommunications, dominates the skyline like a huge phallic symbol of China's economic and technical virility. There are big hotels, money changers, neon signs, supermarkets and nightclubs. An old theatre has been converted into a stock exchange. The economy of the city is in a constant state of boom.

I met with the vice-mayor in a palatial room of a handsome Victorian building on the Bund. Urbane and well informed, he exuded the panache of a seasoned international statesman. Which is what he is. The city's problems, he explained, are problems of growth: more roads, more houses, environmental issues. Australian engineers had helped with some of the water pollution problems. In the Pudong industrial estate we drove past one new factory after another, a gleaming new industrial wasteland. At the estate headquarters building we sat at a big table and were given figures on the number of factories, foreign investors, employees, potential production. 'You speak English with an unusual accent,' I remarked to one of the Chinese across the table.

'Yeah,' he said, 'I'm from Moonee Ponds.' He was spending time in Shanghai advising the Pudong developers how it should be done.

We were taken to see the sights from the top of the newly opened Pearl Tower. A guide explained that the German president would be visiting later in the day. We would be taken up on a trial run. I fumbled for excuses without success. We whistled up seventy-six floors in a crowded lift. Every elevator disaster movie I'd seen flashed into my mind. From the top we looked down on the brown smog of the city.

At meetings businessmen talked about deals, and government officials talked about Chinese market socialism. Exasperated I asked what 'market socialism' meant. 'How do you define it?' There were pauses: whispered conversations. It seemed that the concept emerged clearly in the speeches of Deng Xiaoping.

There's something rather boring about the official presentation of contemporary China. They talk like a bunch of left-wing chartered accountants, infected with the virus of pragmatism. It's all about production, infrastructure, big industrial estates, tall buildings, economic growth. If you admire the talents of the Shanghai Acrobat Company, someone will tell you how much money it makes. If you ask about former Chinese leaders, the question is turned aside. There's not much conversational light and shade, and no apparent sense of history. In fact, there isn't much history. The Chinese Communist Party was founded in Shanghai in 1921. In 1949 the foreign concessions were closed down. Then the history began to be made by Chinese under Mao and his successors. The city began to grow. It produced some of China's greatest leaders, and became the liveliest city in China. But the periods of European commercial and military domination, the Civil War, the Japanese occupation, the golden and decadent years for westerners, the cultural revolution, all seem erased from the history like printed words wiped from a whiteboard.

Bits of the old Shanghai, familiar to westerners, survive. There are older people who must be walking history books. I met one, an elderly gentleman working as a sort of adviser emeritus to a European merchant bank. He was handsome, sprightly, and slightly foppish in the English manner. He wore a tweedy suit that had a Savile Row look about it. A red handkerchief peeped stylishly out of the dress pocket of his jacket. He spoke excellent English. He told me he'd been in Shanghai most of his life. At the time of the Cultural Revolution the Red Guards had kept him at a prison farm for several years. He seemed disinclined to talk about it. A Chinese wall went up.

'Do you remember the 1930s?' I asked.

He gave a big smile. 'Yes,' he said, 'I remember the thirties. I worked for Jardines.'

And there are the physical relics. The Bund is still there, a magnificent nineteenth century boulevard, floodlit at night. The river remains as turbid as ever. The jazz band, famous in the 1930s, still plays in the Peace Hotel with, it's claimed, some of the original members. There are plenty of antique shops and a few old villas. In a westernised hotel you can drink at a 'long bar', aping the famous bar in the Old Shanghai Club. And then there's the House of Dr Sun Yat Sen. Nobody could tell me how to find it.

Going to the Ballet in Japan

The Australian doctor was sitting opposite me at breakfast in a Tokyo hotel. He had a large bowl of All Bran and prunes in front of him, and a second large bowl of fruit. He looked disapprovingly at my poached egg. 'The trouble with this disease,' he was saying, 'is that no one knows about it. People die from it in their sleep. They just stop breathing, old people particularly.' He handed me some off-prints of articles from various medical journals. 'You should read these,' he said, 'it's essential that more people understand the condition.' He looked at me threateningly. 'You may have it yourself.'

'Maybe,' I said, 'it's a good thing. Perhaps it's a good way to go—without knowing.'

He snorted incredulously before deciding I was serious. He changed gear like a Formula One driver in an S bend. 'You have to think of the cost to the country . . . potentially disabled people. It could be bigger than smoking in cost to the health-care system.' I finished my poached egg. 'The problem is ignorance . . . not enough people know about it.' He kept on talking. The All Bran and the prunes and the fruit remained untouched. This man, I thought, will die of executive stress.

My doctor friend was in Japan marketing a medical product for the management of the disorder he had been talking about.

Health is a big issue in Japan. They have a negative birth rate, and an ageing population. By the year 2000, 25 per cent of the population will be over sixty-five. People talk about health. The Japanese staples of fish, rice and vegetables make for a very healthy diet, but it is said to be deficient in calcium. There is concern about osteoporosis, a degenerative bone disease.

The matter came up again in conversation at a gourmet dinner promoting Australian food and wine. I sat next to Mrs Suzuki who runs a cooking school in Tokyo. She had trained in Paris as a cordon bleu cook and was a chevalier of some *Societé des fromages* in France. She spoke English hesitantly, with the slow deliberation of someone searching for words. I was introduced to the world of international culinary buffs. She talked about French, Chinese and Japanese cooking. She liked Taiwanese cooking, particularly game and poultry. 'I travel,' she said, 'to keep up to date. I go to France for the cheese, and I go to Taiwan for the cock. The cock in Taiwan is very good.' I smiled politely. She gave me a quizzical look. 'Wrearly,' she said. 'Don't you beweave me?' Mrs Suzuki hoped that, for health reasons, Japanese people would eat more cheese and other dairy products, 'perhaps from Australia'. She herself was using more cheese in recipes at her classes.

It's not, of course, as if the Japanese were wholly preoccupied with health issues, or that this is all the people talk about. They have had a recession, and Japan's international relations have not been easy. Nor has the big cultural shift springing from generational change. There is the phenomenon of the new, and different sorts of governments led by politicians of a different style from the elderly power brokers of the Liberal Democratic Party who divided the spoils in Japan for over forty years. Old industrialists mumble about the new style of leaders who are less susceptible to factional manipulation and favours from big business. The Japanese people are not great admirers of their politicians. Many of them would like to see a new, more democratic order. So the problems with the Japanese economy and difficult trade relations are an unfriendly mask which hides a deep-seated process of change. At least, most younger Japanese seem to hope so.

A Thai scholar once told me that the countries which will continue to do well in Asia are the ones with a strong and cohesive culture. Japan has its down side, but it remains a cohesive if somewhat formal culture. It has a powerful sense of tradition and continuity. It is changing in its own way.

The Japanese are a polite and hospitable people. Tokyo, with a population of twelve million, must be one of the world's safest cities to walk around in. I was reminded of this one day when I set out to go to the Australian Ballet which was performing in Tokyo. I was running late and took a taxi. The driver misunderstood me and dropped me at a place which didn't seem right. I found myself wandering round a huge market area of downtown Tokyo. I quickly discovered that a dozen words of Japanese don't take you far—certainly not to the ballet. There's a limit to the value of repeating expressions like 'good afternoon', 'how much?', 'thank you', and 'how are you?' to total strangers. They give you odd looks.

Luckily I bumped into an Australian I knew—a twelve million to one chance. He was wearing corduroy trousers and a pullover. I was used to him in a suit. 'What are you dressed like that for?' I shrieked at him hysterically.

'I'm shopping,' he said defensively, and directed me to a metro train.

On the train I showed the man sitting next to me a piece of paper with the name of the theatre written on it. At Ueno Station he tapped me on the shoulder. 'Follow,' he said. He took me out of the station and down the street to the door of the theatre. Then he scurried back to the station to catch the next train home. I slipped into my seat as the curtain went up.

This, it might be said, was an isolated incident, an extraordinary stroke of luck. I don't think so. The traditions of politeness and courtesy are embedded in the culture. It is the old politics and the old ways of doing business which are under some challenge. The consumer benefits of the complex and costly distribution system are increasingly queried. I suspect there is a new openness emerging in the way people talk about their country and its interface with the world.

Japan has more engineers per head of population than any other country, and fewer bean counters than Australia or the United States. Economics is more about people than scrimping an extra dollar of savings. The art of the engineer is obvious in the physical landscape: good buildings, railways, toll roads, bridges and airports. Infrastructure is not a dirty word. In Japan it works and usually it looks good. Engineering and design skills are reflected in the quality of consumer products. Sometimes it is overdone. Understanding bathroom plumbing, for example, is a difficult task. The toilets in the new lounge at Tokyo's Haneda airport are so high-tech that the control panel looks like the flight deck of a Concorde. The lesson for the unsophisticated is not to start anything without knowing how to stop it.

The underlying strength of Japan has always been in its capacity to look ahead, to plan for the next generation of products and people. Now, in different and changing times, they are able to look ahead with a fair degree of confidence about their inherent capacities and high level of skills. With China currently the flavour of the month for many Australian businessmen, it would be a terrible mistake to overlook the importance of Japan. We have a long-standing trading relationship with Japan. Japanese perceptions of Australian capacities are improving. A number of Australian high-tech companies are now doing business successfully in the Japanese market: a drop in the ocean, but ten times the number of a few years ago. Compared with my first time in Japan in 1983, the Australian presence is competent and sophisticated. The present Australian ambassador in Tokyo is the first to speak fluent Japanese. There are now many more professional Japanese-speaking Australians working in Japan. The opportunities for understanding the marketplace and the society are better than ever. The more we get on the front foot in taking those opportunities, the better the long-term relationship will be.

The time I went to the Australian Ballet, both it and Yothu Yindi were performing to packed and enthusiastic audiences. The Japanese respond to quality and excellence. Historically, we've been recognised for good coal, iron ore, and some agricultural products. Nowadays it's increasingly things like ice cream and other food products, software and innovative high-tech equipment. The ballet and Yothu Yindi are a bonus. Understanding and selling to Japan, of course, require persistence as well. It's a place where carpetbaggers need not apply. As I left Tokyo, I thought about my doctor friend. He had persistence and a good product, successful in many countries. I'm sure in time he'll do well in Japan. I recalled him diagnosing a public health problem with words which might describe the changing nature of Japan: 'The problem is ignorance; it's essential that more people understand.'

To Which Country Are You Ambassador?

The chemist handed me a large bottle of antibiotics: the ones designed to fix the plague. He shook his head gravely, indicating that you wouldn't catch him going to India. I was advised to take two of the tablets immediately if I met a plague suspect. My doctor friend, the one with the personal breathalyser in his car, told me I should take some surgical masks to wear in plague-infected areas. He told me if I phoned his secretary she would provide some for me. He's quite unrealistic in some ways, but always tries to be helpful. He's an agnostic, but seems to worry about my soul as well as my body. For a moment I was attracted by his idea. A mask might improve my appearance. I enjoyed a fleeting fantasy of my blue eyes darting out from above the mask, like Ali Baba or Lawrence of Arabia.

In the end I rejected the idea. I might frighten children, or people might think I had bad breath.

I arrived in Madras in the middle of the night. I was suffering from a cold, picked up in Melbourne, which produced the same symptoms as the early stages of the plague: a heavy head, sneezing and congestion of the chest. I wondered if I'd be regarded as a suspect. Indeed, how could they tell? How could I tell myself? At the immigration counter the official examined my passport closely. He glanced up at me. 'To which country are you ambassador?' he asked.

'Australia,' I said.

'No, no, no. You are from Australia. To which country are you ambassador?'

'Roving ambassador,' I replied.

'Roving,' he said. 'Where is roving? It is not, I think, a place.'

I gave a more detailed explanation. 'Ah,' he said, 'it is moving. Now this is something we have got to know.' He smiled wearily, and stamped the passport.

I wondered if he was a plague suspect. Should I take a couple of tablets, just in case?

India is a country of approximately nine hundred million people of whom about sixty died of the plague at the time I was there. In the state of Rajasthan, somewhere between 1000 and 4000 people (depending on whether you believed the BBC or Indian newspapers) died of malaria in the same period. The plague outbreak was the first recorded in India for twenty-eight years. Though the statistics are unreliable, it is probable that in those years more people died of bubonic plague in the United States than in India. It is a universal disease.

In western culture, malaria is accepted as a disease which people get in the tropics. If proper medical attention is available it can be cured. But it lurks in the consciousness as an illness which kills large numbers of people in tropical countries. It's like heart attacks or the road toll in wealthy societies with a temperate climate. The plague, however, invokes horror and a tendency to panic. It's as if we remembered it from the middle ages. It makes us feel good to think we've put it behind us. In fact, like malaria, it can be cured with proper medical attention: something which is not always available in the villages and crowded cities of India.

India's population is still increasing by about eighteen million a year. It is a poor country with inadequate community services like health care and education. Government-sponsored attempts to control the birth rate have largely failed. The long-term solution is now seen to be in raising educational standards. It is an awesome task.

There has been, however, a new dynamism in India in the 1990s. The economy is growing, business is booming, the airlines are busy, and foreign investment is pouring into the country. Much of the credit for this has to go to the government in power between 1991 and 1996 under Prime Minister Rao, assisted by an able finance minister, Mr Singh. In 1991 it began to introduce measures to reduce the mass of bureaucratic regulation which had stifled the economy and business initiative. The results have been quite dramatic, and the trend towards a more open vigorous economy is probably irreversible. Once a sensible, popularly supported strategy is developed, it's hard for politicians to mess it up. India's capable entrepreneurial class has an unprecedented degree of optimism about the future. There is an air of confidence, a feeling that the country is moving, and in the right direction. And whilst it may not yet be apparent to the poor of India, amongst the elites of business and the top rank of government officials there are exciting plans for improving infrastructure and services. Their enthusiasm rubs off on foreign businessmen and women. German, Korean and Singaporean businesses are investing in infrastructure projects, manufacturing and service industries. Singapore is building a high-tech village in Bangalore. There are a handful of Australian companies in India, representing a drop in an ocean of opportunities. Too few Australians have caught the new mood of a country with which we share a common language, similar institutions and a common business culture. Too many are deterred by perceptions from the past. Nonetheless Australia's better companies are there investing and looking for opportunities.

India is a place where perceptions of the past are rich and constantly reinforced. The 'Afghan' Church in Bombay bears its name because it was the parish church for British regiments stationed in the city in the late nineteenth century. From there they went off to fight on the northern frontiers of India and in the fierce and bloody Afghan wars. Today it seldom functions as a church. A small boy unlocks the rusty gates to let you in. There is an air of decay. The walls and battle flags tell the story: memorials to death in battle in Afghanistan, and death in Bombay from malaria, typhoid, cholera and the plague.

Until 1947 the ex-pats in India were the soldiers of the Queen. In today's India the growing number of ex-pats are businessmen. The modern adventurers are the tourists from various countries in Europe and the Middle East. They come in big numbers, but at the time of the overblown plague scare there were very few from France and Germany. Like their forebears, however, British tourists were still in evidence. I kept bumping into groups of Brits on the wrong side of middle-age—optimistic and energetic tourists led by intrepid women who reminded me of Joyce Grenfell and Margaret Rutherford, with men like Wilfred Hyde White following a couple of paces behind. 'Not many French tourists here,' remarked a Wilfred Hyde White with a sardonic smile, across the breakfast table in a Rajasthan hotel. He was enjoying old continental rivalries and the sentimental attachment the British have for India's past. 'Mad Dogs and Englishmen' must, I thought, have been his favourite song.

Enjoying a drink in the magnificent courtyard of a Maharani's palace partly converted into a hotel, I was startled by the skirl of bagpipes in a nearby courtyard. I went over to have a look. It was the band of the Maharani's palace guards in kilts and full military regalia. They play every night at 7.30. When they finished playing, the band members lined up ready for the order to march away. The drum major moved down the line carrying a small tray of food. He moulded a ball of the food with his fingers and popped one into the mouth of each of the bandsmen. He came over to me. I must have looked apprehensive, fearing a hot chilli. 'Don't worry,' he said, 'the food has been blessed.' In fact it tasted like raw pastry mixed with sugar. It is an ancient custom symbolising security and a bright future: something of which India is entitled to be confident.

Dobradjin, Dosvadanya

It was about two years ago in the city of Hue, the ancient capital of Vietnam. We'd been to a restaurant for dinner, and were riding back to our hotel in cyclos, about six in a group, each of us travelling in a separate cyclo. It was after 10 p.m. and the streets of Hue were winding and dark.

As we passed under a street light at an intersection, a group of kids on bikes rode up alongside shouting at us with great excitement and hilarity. My doctor friend, the one with the personalised breathalyser in his Melbourne car, was in the cyclo alongside mine. In some ways he's absurdly impractical: a bit of a boffin. I once heard him lecturing a Ho Chi Minh City cyclo driver with six kids on the importance of a population policy. The cyclo driver hardly spoke English, but he listened patiently. On this occasion my friend entered into the spirit of it all. 'Young man,' he shouted back to one of the cyclists, 'we may look incongruous, we may seem inebriated, but my God we are not irrelevant.' The kids didn't understand these profound utterances, but clearly thought they were very funny. I'm still trying to work out why. Maybe they knew something.

A cyclo is a three-wheeled contraption with a rider up front, and a seat like an unpadded armchair for the passenger at the back. While the driver pedals away, the passenger sits back and enjoys the view, and the passing fantasy of belonging to the leisured, unworking class. Cyclos, or their equivalents, are a common feature of poor countries in Asia. As countries get richer, cyclos tend to disappear and be replaced by taxis. It is not always progress. The machines which replace manpower clog up the streets, pollute the atmosphere and create noise. A cyclo ride is an arrangement which has to be negotiated. The driver bargains until he gets a good deal, maybe two or three dollars an hour. The passenger from a wealthy country thinks he's got a good deal too. It's all to do with exchange rates, and relative standards of living.

I love travelling in cyclos, although sometimes I have a twinge of the guilt of European colonial history, and ponder why the driver's doing all the work and I'm doing nothing. Then I recall a poem written by the Marxist street poet, Paul Potts. He wrote poetry in the 1950s and sold it in the streets of London. Perhaps one day he'll be rediscovered. His whole life was politically incorrect. He wrote a poem called 'The Nerve of the Bitch':

> She sips her dry martini
> Darkies sweat and white man's curses are in the cocktail shaker
> The nerve of the Bitch;
> She thinks because we're always pulling loads, we're donkeys.

In a cyclo, positioned as it were somewhere between the bitch and the cyclo driver, I sometimes find myself thinking about Paul Potts' poem. Then I remind myself that it's all about exchange rates and technology transfer, and that there is a plausible explanation for everything.

A cyclo, like a taxi, is a private sector extension of the public transport system. When you negotiate a price with a cyclo driver and climb into the passenger seat, you put yourself entirely in his hands. You don't know the best route to your destination, and unless you have a few words of a common language, explanations are impossible. The driver may chat away, but you don't know what he's saying. It's quite relaxing listening to him. Fortunately they seem to know where they're going. In a taxi in Sydney or Melbourne you sometimes pay a lot more for comparable adventures.

Not long after returning from Vietnam, I took a cab from Sydney airport to the city. The driver was a dark swarthy young man, close to being handsome. I gave him an address in George Street, and he dived into the glove box for his street directory. 'Don't worry,' I said, 'I know where to go.'

He had his driver's identification photo stuck on the dashboard. 'Some people say I look like Al Pacino,' he said. 'What do you think?' I said he looked a bit like Al Pacino. He told me he came from the Middle East and had been in the army. When he wasn't driving a cab, he taught kung fu. He took another dive into the glove box and produced a brochure. It said, 'Learn to Protect Yourself. All ages, shapes and sizes—male and female. Enquire *now*. Don't put it off, it may be too late!!' While we chatted he kept glancing at me. It made me nervous. He seemed to be sizing me up. 'I've worked out who you are,' he pronounced after about ten minutes. I tried a quizzical smile.

'You are,' he said, 'an old actor?'—a pretty wounding remark to make to a former politician.

'No, no,' I protested vehemently.

'Yes you are. You were the boxing trainer in the film *Rocky*.'

'No,' I said firmly, 'that was somebody else.'

He smiled knowingly. 'You can't fool me,' he said. As I got out of the cab he invited me to come to his kung fu class. 'In the next film you can be a kung fu trainer.'

When I got back to Melbourne the same afternoon I opened the door of the first cab at the airport rank. I recognised the driver as someone who'd driven me a couple of months before. I recalled the fact that he was Russian. '*Dosvadanya*,' I shouted at him cheerily.

Unfortunately he didn't remember me. He looked startled,

like an old actor confronted by a maniac. 'Vat for,' he said, 'you say goodbye to me before you get in zee cab? Vat are you trying to do?'

I sensed we were at cross purposes. I started to babble incoherently. 'Don't you remember me? I remember you . . . you come from Siberia and you were born in the Ukraine, just near the Rumanian border.' He looked even more startled. 'Don't you remember me showing you the quickest way to get to East Melbourne from the airport?'

His eyes lit up. 'Ah,' he said, 'East Melbourne! Yes, I remember. Now I will take you to East Melbourne.' On the drive in from Tullamarine he gave me a short course in the Russian language. He taught me to say '*Dobradjin*', which means 'good day', and which was what I intended to say to him in the first place. Learning a few words of Russian seemed like kung fu: a useful means of self defence.

I got out of the cab in the city. The driver and I parted firm friends. 'We'll always have East Melbourne,' I said—a bit, I realised later, like Ingrid Bergman in *Casablanca*.

'*Dosvadanya*,' he replied. It had been a long day. I opted for the public sector and caught a tram home. It cost two dollars. It felt a very normal thing to do and, like a cyclo driver in his home country, the Vietnamese tram driver seemed to know exactly where he was going.

L'Oiseau Dep Lam

My hotel in Hanoi is four storeys high with three guest rooms on each floor. It's the width of a small Victorian terrace. There is no lift. So after breakfast I sometimes trudge up the stairs behind a stout French woman built like a Henry Moore statue. There may, I think, be aerodynamic benefits. For one reason or another it makes the climb seem easier. I'm in Room 301 on the third floor, which costs about forty dollars a night and has a balcony overlooking the street. The room has the well-polished look of a millionaire's yacht. It's bright and comfortable. A notice on the wall headed 'Regulations for Guests' tells me that 'due to health and hazar regulations cooking are not allowed in room' and 'any exploisive materials or flammable are prohibited'. It sounds bureaucratic. But it's reassuring. I hope the guy in 201 has read it carefully.

I keep stepping out onto the balcony. Opposite there's a row of higgledy piggledy terraces of all shapes and sizes. They have TV dishes on the roofs. Washing hangs on makeshift lines. I try and guess the number of people in each house from the clothes on the line. On the street below, a family of four sits at a small table eating their dinner. It looks enticing: steamed crabs, noodles, big fleshy mangoes. From time to time fresh dishes are brought out from inside the house. Opposite, a barber is doing brisk business on the footpath. He has a mirror stuck to a wall, a stool, and a small box with scissors and clippers. Low overheads.

The street buzzes with noise. The dominant sound is of scooters, just like Rome. The traffic is a nightmare and a miracle. Pushbikes with loads meant for a semi-trailer, pedestrians, women carrying huge burdens on shoulder poles, motorbikes, scooters, horse-drawn carts, minibuses, and shouting street vendors. It's a dramatic mixture of old and new technologies.

The hotel breakfast is continental, a French legacy. Mango juice, bread rolls, and coffee strong enough to set off a pacemaker. As I eat, a canary is trilling away vigorously in the next room: a real songster, like Schwarzkopf singing Schubert's 'Trout'. '*Dep lam*,' I say to the young woman pouring the coffee. 'Very beautiful.' She blushes, flutters her eyelids, and gives me an embarrassed smile. I'm talking about the canary, but she thinks I'm being fresh. I try to recover. '*L'oiseau. 'L'oiseau dep lam*,' I stammer in a sort of eastern suburbs Esperanto. It doesn't seem to work. Another crazy foreigner.

I used to come here on official visits. I stayed first at the Vietnamese government's state guest house. It was certainly official. But basic. There were rumours of rats in the rooms, which pinched your socks in the night. On subsequent visits I stayed at the Metropole, a French-owned, stylish and expensive oasis for foreign visitors. From cars and hotels and government buildings I looked out at Hanoi through plate-glass windows. I recall the city as being poorer and less lively.

One official visit was much like another: a cavalcade of cars from the airport along narrow roads cluttered with buffalo, pushbikes, pedestrians, horse-drawn carts, geese and pigs. In Hanoi there were official banquets and meetings with ministers in crowded rooms, exchanging information and bureaucratic pleasantries. I remember languid fans beating hopelessly in the humid air. Conversations were conducted through interpreters. Wreaths had to be ceremonially laid at the Museum of Ho Chi Minh. There were discussions with the prime minister in the magnificent presidential palace. My official host was a minister in his early seventies, who'd spent thirty-six years in the army. He'd fought against the Japanese, the French, the Chinese and Americans. He looked fit and purposeful, a symbolic survivor of the history of Hanoi. Not many foreigners were in town. In the streets children waved at the car and shouted, '*Lien Xo*' (Russians). Times were tough, and so were the people who had endured forty years of war. My most vivid memory is of children sitting in the middle of a roadway intersection, doing their homework by the overhead street light. There was no electricity at home.

This time I went down-market, seeking a kerbside view. For a hundred dollars at the airport money exchange I was given a bundle of notes the size of a brick. 'That's a million,' the man said as he put the brick on the counter. I felt conspicuously wealthy. I stuffed it inside my jacket and pushed my way nervously through the crowd. A taxi took me along a big new freeway into Hanoi: the animals, bikes and carts had gone, pushed from the freeway into distant shapes on the horizon.

Down-market there are no cars, no official banquets, and no interpreters. But nowadays there are taxis, good restaurants, and quite a few people who speak some English and French. The Vietnamese language is a bigger challenge. I have lessons from the three young women who come to clean my room in the hotel. My pronunciation sends them into fits of laughter. Vietnamese is a tonal language. The alphabet is the same as English. The grammar is relatively simple. It's the pronunciation which makes you nervous. A short word like *ma* can mean six different things including 'mother' and 'horse', depending on the intonation. So it could be dangerous if you get the sound wrong. *Nam* means 'man' or 'five'. If you say it with an Australian accent, and it sounds like *nem*, it means 'pickled raw pork': bad news if you're trying to describe the gender of the Iranian ambassador. Sometimes it's best to rely on sign language, supplemented with a touch of French and universal expressions like 'OK'. My wife, who speaks more Vietnamese than I do, seems to communicate better. A natural thespian, she turns away street vendors with gestures and words like 'No more postcards today, dahling', while I'm struggling to pronounce the Vietnamese word for 'no'.

If you avoid the holes in the footpaths and the motorbikes avoid you, Hanoi is a safe city to walk around. It's a great place for gawking. The streets of the old city buzz with commerce like a hundred Victoria Markets on a busy day. In the official quarter I found myself peering through the heavy iron gates of the presidential palace. 'I've been there,' I thought to myself. Outside the mausoleum I wondered if Ho Chi Minh would approve of all this cosmopolitan activity. I rather think he would. Poverty remains the lot of many of the citizens of this city. But it lacks the abject and hopeless character of poverty in some other countries. There is a sense of optimism and well-being. Hanoians seem a laid-back, smiling lot.

It's the mixtures of ancient and new technologies and of cultural influences which make Hanoi a fascinating place. The Chinese occupied this city for nearly a thousand years. The French were here for more than a century. Later the Russians had a more subtle presence for three decades. They have all been and gone. There's a Chinese legacy of pagodas and temples, and a touch of Confucianism. The boulevards, the opera house, bread sticks, and fine colonial villas are reminders of the French. The Russians bequeathed some 'Soviet Brutal' architecture, and a legacy of bureaucracy. All this has been absorbed into a dominant Vietnamese culture. The people of Hanoi seem patient and resilient. Now there is a new invasion: consumer goods from China, a 'foreign legion' of French tourists picking over the past, businessmen in smart suits from wealthy Asian countries and Europe, doing deals in the lounge of the Metropole Hotel. In time, I suspect, these influences will be absorbed as well.

I sneaked into the Metropole for a cappuccino. It seemed like a compromise. I walked happily back to my own hotel. The family next door were having their dinner on the footpath. I stopped to look for a few seconds and was offered some soup. The barber had packed up and gone home. A man dressed like the commissionaire at the Paris Ritz opened the hotel door, greeting me in French. As I climbed the stairs I worked out that in that little hotel he'd probably only open the door about ten times a day. Low productivity and good service.

In a restaurant one evening I talked with two Australian women tourists about their first impressions. They seemed captivated by the sometimes dramatically beautiful countryside and friendly people. They were disturbed by the signs of poverty. 'And yet,' one said, 'everybody seems happy. There's always someone looking after the children: a big sister or brother or a grandfather.' They noticed a sense of community. Maybe, one suggested, Australians were not so rich after all.

Toasted Cheese in Harry's Bar

It was my first morning in Venice for nearly ten years. I was sitting at a table in Harry's Bar. I'd ordered a cappuccino and a toasted cheese sandwich. There were four middle-aged Italian women sitting up at the bar, talking about their teenage kids, how they watched too much television and neglected their homework. It sounded familiar, like morning tea in a shopping mall at home. There were no other customers. I'd expected something a bit different. In fact, in my wildest imaginings, I thought a few of the old-time regulars might be there: people like Hemingway, and Scott Fitzgerald, and Henry Miller. I could have offered to buy them a drink, an aperitif of some kind: perhaps a Pernod with a bit of water to make it go cloudy. It would have been worth it, just to get the opportunity to hear about the old times, and to ask a few questions. Scott Fitzgerald would still have interesting views about how to run a party. Hemingway might have changed his mind about the gun lobby. I could have asked Henry Miller if he'd ever been accused of sexual harassment.

These questions might have tossed them a bit. But the surroundings would have been totally familiar. The polished wooden tables and chairs with comfortable brown leather cushions, the friendly and highly professional waiters in white jackets, the faded framed drawings dated 1935 on the walls and the cosiness of the place had, I suspect, not changed at all. Like Venice itself, Harry's Bar is full of history. The receipt for my coffee and sandwich had 'Harry's Bar—since 1931' written in the top corner. Those faded Apache dancers in the drawings on the wall had seen a thing or two over the years.

Italy in 1931 was witnessing the rise and rise of Mussolini. The fall was a long way ahead. In contrast to his successors he had a long time in politics. The day I sat in Harry's Bar, the Italians had just elected yet another new government. Mussolini's grand-daughter was part of it, together with 105 colleagues from the neo-fascist Italian Social Movement, called the National Alliance. Gianfranco Fini, the leader of another party called the National Alliance, had wasted no time in praising Mussolini as 'the greatest statesman of the century'. The Alliance, however, was only part of the new right-wing majority in the 650-seat lower house of the Italian parliament. The other parts were the Northern League, an organisation led by the charismatic Umberto Bossi, and Forza Italia, a collection of right-wing yuppies led by Silvio Berlusconi.

The Northern League has a secessionist flavour about it. Northerners don't like their taxes being spent on the more impoverished provinces of southern Italy. Forza Italia was not really a political party at all. It was more of an advertising stunt. Berlusconi controlled a huge business empire embracing construction, insurance, chain stores, newspapers, three television channels, film houses, and the highly successful Milan soccer team. He seemed a bit like Alan Bond in the late 1980s. It was alleged that his business conglomerates were heavily in debt. The magistrates investigating corruption were sniffing at the heels of his business confreres. But he had a bit of a cult following. He was seen as a man who opens doors, gets things done, crashes through. Election watchers round the world are familiar with the type. For a while they seem a refreshing change from dithering politicians. Mussolini had the same sort of charm. He made the trains run on time.

In Harry's Bar I thumbed through *Il Gazzettino*, a Venice newspaper, trying to understand the meaning of the election results. I was also trying to look at home in the place. I suspected the shrewd-looking head waiter had a sense of *déjà vu* about me. He'd summed me up as an arts graduate from some red-brick, Anglo-Saxon university, an incurable romantic with not much money, trying to recapture the past: the world of Hemingway, Scott Fitzgerald and Henry Miller. The newspaper was full of the triumphs of the candidates of the Northern League. They were all pictured in boxed-in paragraphs like Italian funeral notices. In each box there was a photo, the occupation of the successful candidate, the number of votes won and, of all things, the type of car each candidate drove. I imagined them in their Fiats, Peugeots, Lamborghinis and BMWs all pouring down the autostrada to the parliament in Rome. Surely, I thought, there will be an accident. But I had no real reason to think that. Like everybody else reading *Il Gazzettino* that morning, I had no hard information on which to make a judgment.

Italians are a serious, talented people. They'd like their politicians and their governments to be taken seriously too. That has usually been difficult. Perhaps they thought it would be different this time. But I doubted it. The new government was such an awkward coalition of political groups. Apart from the neo-fascists, there was a flavour of amateurism about them, and too much enthusiasm, the inevitable precursor of disillusionment. It had all happened because Italian politics, like nature, abhors a vacuum. The traditional Italian right, which had governed in one alliance or another since the 1950s, had been totally discredited by revelations of bribery and corruption. The vacuum had been filled by a strange alliance with an unclear image. I thought of a Milan businessman who once told me that Italians were good at solving a crisis. 'That is why,' he said, 'we keep on creating them. So that they can be solved.' In Italian politics, time is a great healer of over-optimism.

Outside Harry's Bar I stopped pondering Italian politics. The spring sunshine sparkled on the Grand Canal. Small boats were bobbing at their moorings, fixed with metal rings to the stone footpath. Venice was going about its business as usual. The tourist season was beginning. It was the right time to visit, before the summer invasion clogged the streets. The stylish boutiques were ready for it, with the latest and best which Italy and Europe could provide. A smart-looking Japanese lady darted in and out of fashion shops with a pocket calculator at the ready. In a discreet stone doorway of a narrow, cobbled street I discovered the latest in bank machines. I managed to persuade it to spew out a wad of lira in exchange for the Mastercard. In Venice the newest technology and ancient craftsmanship sit stylishly together. I found a friend gazing dreamily into the window of a bakery and cake shop. In the narrow street, the scent of the cake shop was powerful and seductive. I retreated into a nearby archway, on which a graffiti artist had written 'time is measured in opportunities lost'—a signal, I thought, to forgo the temptations of the flesh, and walk the streets of Venice,

Those narrow cobbled streets contain more magical urban delights than any other place on earth: stone pedestrian bridges built by craftsmen, handsome old buildings juxtaposed with water, tiny piazzas with market stalls and cafe umbrellas, the famous Venetian blondes sipping Campari in the sun. And it is all complemented by the sounds of Venice: footfalls on the cobblestones and the trundling wheels of hand-drawn carts. The city is a unique experience. The motor car does not intrude here: no horns, no fumes, no traffic lights, no risks. It is quite un-Italian.

In Piazza San Marco the pigeons vied with history as the main attraction. Tame and fat, they posed for pictures like medieval Venetian courtiers. Strutting and cooing they stuffed themselves with crusts of bread. Under the colonnades, surrounding the square, the tourists stuffed themselves with pasta and watched the pigeons. One sensed it had been going on a long time: different people, different pigeons, the same cobblestones and the same proud buildings.

In the gloom of the cathedral tourists huddled together in groups, listening reverently as their guides explained the mysteries of the Italian Renaissance in German, Japanese, English and French. Earnestness transcended the language differences. They were intent on getting value for money. Eavesdropping, I learnt that the great Venetian painter Titian lived to the age of ninety-nine. Perhaps, I thought, it was the lifestyle: all that pasta, and sea air, and those voluptuous models. Other tourists preferred to do it on their own, a thing like a telephone pressed to their ear, pacing the floor, locked into an electronic monologue on art and religious history. Again they looked earnest, frantically absorbing useless information, candidates for surfing the Internet.

In my hotel room the sound of a gondolier singing 'Funiculi Funicula' floated upwards in the still air and through the open window. I looked down at the gondolas gliding past on the canal below, a Japanese honeymoon couple in one, some noisy Americans in another. The singer had a full load of Chinese passengers in his boat, clapping their hands in time to the music, the vanguard of the next wave of tourist invaders.

On my walks I found a place where medieval executions were carried out. I found the old Jewish Quarter: the original ghetto, the home of the great metal foundries of the sixteenth century. And on the wall of a house I read a commemorative plaque marking the spot where the former owner had been shot by an SS firing squad fifty years ago. Venice, for hundreds of years the capital of a great sea-going empire, where merchants were princes, and architects and craftsmen built with confidence and style, seemed to absorb all these things. The city has seen it all before, and survived as a monument to human ingenuity. No wonder it's business as usual. All those new politicians with their mug shots in the newspaper, driving their noisy cars down the autostrada to Rome, somehow seemed rather grubby. This place would continue to outshine them all.

Coachman, Stop. The Postilion Has Fallen Off.

I keep turning up in Rome like a bad penny. I've never quite worked out why. It's not because it's called 'The Eternal City'. I'm not particularly addicted to all those statues of disabled people missing an arm or a leg or in some cases a head. Those cold-looking men with muscles like Arnold Schwarzenegger and punched-in noses evoke neither pity nor admiration. I'm able to tolerate only a limited number of churches in one day. It's nerve-wracking leaping out of the way of motor scooters, and irritating to have to push and shove with other tourists in the Sistine Chapel.

Perhaps I like Rome for a different reason. The first time I went there I was young and in love. Looking back, of course, I'm not sure why. Perhaps it was a meeting of two cultures.

She was English. She talked posh and reminded me of Nancy Mitford. Her name was Penelope. She liked my Australian accent. I had something going for me. She was also very funny—eccentric in an English way. So we threw coins in the Trevi Fountain, buzzed around on a scooter, and stood on 'tippy toes' to watch the coronation of a Pope. She told me her daddy wouldn't approve of me. This seemed to make me more attractive.

Later she married an Anglican vicar and disappeared from my life, though she's still in *Debrett's Peerage*. The vicarage I can imagine as an ecclesiastical Fawlty Towers. She should have married Manuel the waiter. He has a strange accent and her daddy wouldn't have approved of him either.

Alone, or in the wrong mood, the finest city can be a dismal place. Rome is an exception. It submerges you in a stream of human history. You feel part of something. I decided to go back. In Australia Paul Keating was prime minister. John Hewson was leader of the opposition. Politics looked like business as usual. I was no longer part of that. It was time for something different. Rome seemed a logical place to go. It was anonymous, different, and part of Europe's oldest mainstream.

As the plane approached Rome's Fumincino airport, the Qantas flight attendant came up to me. 'Some of the other passengers asked me what you're doing in Rome,' he said. 'I told them you're buying a couple of suits for Paul Keating, and some spare parts for John Hewson's Ferrari.'

'Thank you,' I replied. 'I'm afraid neither of those blokes would trust me with such a sensitive mission.' I couldn't help thinking the man had style. If I'd heard the remark in the jungles of the Amazon, I'd still have picked him as a Qantas steward, with his images of Italy drawn from glossy magazines, and his easy political satire. It's like racism or sexism. It should be called 'politicism'—a new Australian word, another example of the politically incorrect. Politicians get the people they deserve.

What did I do in Rome? Well, I stayed in a small hotel in

a narrow cobbled street. Apart from the scooters, it probably hadn't changed in three hundred years. My room was two floors up in a groaning lift the size of a phone box. When I opened the shutters in the morning, the springtime sunshine and the sounds of the city flooded through the window. It was a small room with a wicker chair. It reminded me of Van Gogh's room at Arles. At times I imagined I was Van Gogh—usually in his saner, more creative period. Although, when the scooters revved up in the street below, I contemplated cutting off both ears. Either way it was a short-lived fantasy. I once won third prize in a Warrnambool Art Show for a drawing called 'Still Life in the Senate'—but the truth is, I can't paint.

Being practical and a sucker for authenticity, I hung my washing out the window on a long pole. There was no hassle. I could sit and watch my socks dry. A brochure on the table told me that Stendahl, Mazzini and Garibaldi stayed in this hotel. I wondered what they did here. I imagined Garibaldi putting his muddy boots on the window sill to dry, Mazzini dreaming political dreams of a united Italy. Stendahl, I couldn't imagine—perhaps a courting couple clopped by in a horse-drawn carriage and gave him an idea.

Rome is a great place for fantasies. There are no high-rise buildings in the inner city. It is a place of human scale, buzzing with the life of the streets. Roman taxi drivers imagine they are Fangio. Men, strolling in the evening, glance at their reflections in the shop windows thinking, one suspects, that they are not unlike Marcello Mastroianni. Elegantly dressed young women glide past, imagining themselves perhaps as future Sophia Lorens; not, I couldn't help noticing, without some justification.

Fantasies, I suspect, are best conducted in anonymity. I thought I'd achieved this. Then, in an unguarded moment, gazing up at the dome of the Pantheon and marvelling at early Roman ingenuity, I found myself surrounded by a tour group of senior citizens from Sydney, talking excitedly as if, in the heart of Rome, they'd suddenly found a prehistoric man. The thought made me nervous. Dressed in fluorescent green t-shirts, they looked like retired lollipop ladies from children's crossings in the outer suburbs. To put their identity beyond doubt, their t-shirts were embossed in front with the words 'I am Australian' and at the back with 'So am I'. You had to walk round them to get the full message. 'I'm going to tell my husband I saw you,' one said as if I'd been caught in compromising circumstances.

'You're a pimp,' I muttered under my breath.

The kindly lollipop ladies somehow upset me. For a moment I felt a prisoner of my past, so I fled the Pantheon, and headed for the Church of Santa Maria della Concepzione. I wanted to get things in perspective. It was the place to go. In the crypt of the church you can, for a small fee, view the bones and skulls of four thousand Capuchin monks, accumulated over the centuries. It's 'alas poor Yorick' on a massive scale: a good place for reflection. I'd been there a few times before. It brought me, as they say, back to earth. I set out on a long walk.

At the Coliseum I marvelled at the ingenuity of the builders of ancient Rome. They built to impress emperors, with a trickle-down effect for tourists. It has lasted for nearly 2000 years. They understood geometry and created the first intelligent buildings. Their knowledge of acoustics, displayed in theatres and amphitheatres, was almost high-tech. They were less sensitive about spectator sports. In the Coliseum, on a good day, a lot of bears, lions, tigers, slaves and gladiators would be slaughtered. There were no injury lists: only fatalities. The Coliseum looks so much smaller than the MCG. But, at the equivalent of a Grand Final, it housed sixty thousand spectators. Roman senators had reserved seats in the front row. Their names are still there, carved in stone. The corporate box is older than we think.

Towards evening, loitering in the Piazza di Spagna, I watched the crowds of tourists, going slowly up and quickly down the majestic Spanish Steps. In the half light I noticed what looked like a phosphorescent cloud amongst the darkly clothed tourists, descending to the piazza. It seemed threatening, like chemicals escaping from a nuclear reactor. Just in time I realised what it was. It was the lollipop ladies in their fluorescent t-shirts.

I slipped quickly into the Keats and Shelley Museum, a three-storey Victorian terrace which sits conveniently at the corner of the Spanish Steps and the piazza. It's a nice house, furnished in the style to which John Keats would have been accustomed. The curator, a tweedy English academic, matched the furniture. The place was full of old manuscripts, and story boards describing the life and death of Keats, who died in the house in 1821. He was twenty-six. His friend Percy Bysshe Shelley wrote 'Adonais', a lament for Keats, a few months later. Shelley drowned the following year, aged thirty. Another friend, Lord Byron, died two years later at the ripe old age of thirty-six. These three were a wild and talented bunch. Shelley wrote his first novel when he was sixteen. At twenty-two, Keats was confident enough to say, 'I think that when I come to die, I shall be amongst the English poets.' In his letters Byron recalls his early fondness for making love and swimming. 'But now,' he wrote at thirty-two, 'as I never swim unless I tumble into the water, I don't make love until I am obliged.'

Browsing in the Keats and Shelley Museum is a bit depressing. It makes you think you've wasted your time. It's also a reminder of the nineteenth century invasion of Italy by the English literati. Apart from Keats, Shelley and Byron, Coleridge, Thackeray, Leigh Hunt, Ruskin, Robert Browning and Elizabeth Browning spent part of their lives in Italy. Browning summed it up with a piece of doggerel:

> Open my heart, and you will see
> Graved inside of it, Italy.

Perhaps Italy provided freedom from the constraints of English society. The sunshine and antiquities were a bonus. In fact, the country was a favourite stamping-ground for the English upper classes. On my own first visit, Penelope carried a nineteenth-century English-Italian phrase book borrowed from her grandfather's library. It was full of useful expressions like 'Coachman, stop. The postilion has fallen off.' and 'You insolent fellow. Take me at once to the British Consulate'.

Over the centuries Rome seems to have absorbed human eccentricities with some compassion. It turns a benign eye on venal sins. Mostly it's a tolerant place. Romans enjoy life without expecting too much—but this decade the tolerance of the *Popolo Romano* has not extended to their politicians. The level of scepticism about the Italian political system is enormous. People spend a lot of time talking about it.

A barber told me he paid too much tax, and was ripped off by corrupt politicians and businessmen. 'In a year's time,' he pronounced gloomily, 'Italy will be like Yugoslavia.' He was, I suspect, an unduly pessimistic man. On my first visit to Italy in the late 1950s, as our ship sailed into the Bay of Naples, I remember asking a man standing next to me at the ship's rail whether the communists would take power in Italy. 'Never,' he said confidently, 'the Pope won't let them.' In a sense he was right. For forty years the art of winning government in Italian politics was the art of keeping the communists out. It required odd compromises, and strange alliances. Now that unifying historic pressure has disappeared. Like champagne when the cork is clumsily removed, the politics of Italy is bubbling over. It's turned out to be a poor vintage.

The Italian political system, which Italians have lived with since World War II, has fallen on hard times. Nothing new you might think: but this time it is different. More than 150 of Italy's 600 members of parliament have been cited by magistrates for various forms of corruption. There are many fallen idols in the business community. Amongst the politicians former Socialist prime minister Bettino Craxi shared the spoils amongst his colleagues, and became very unpopular. Crowds pelted coins at him: tainted money. Prosecutions loomed. He now lives in self-imposed exile. A godfather of Italian politics,

Giulio Andreotti, has been accused of long-standing involvement with the Mafia, and is now the principal defendant in a marathon criminal trial.

Over the years Andreotti was prime minister seven times and held numerous ministerial portfolios. He mixed in the salons of world politics. In the Italian political cauldron, he kept bobbing, like a cork, to the top. Scarcely charismatic, he was the master of compromise, the great political survivor. In her memoirs Margaret Thatcher described him as a politician who 'seemed to have a positive aversion to principle, even a conviction that a man of principle was doomed to be a figure of fun.' Such political types exist: few have survived for so long.

I first met Andreotti in his gloomy office in his hotel in Rome. The man who showed me in looked like a butler in a haunted castle. Andreotti wore, I remember, a shabby grey cardigan, which reminded me of Labor politicians of the Calwell era, when cardigans were the distinctive mark of the white collar worker. There were no Italian suits then. We had a pleasant talk around a variety of subjects. Politeness forbade me asking, 'Mr Andreotti, how have you survived so long? Shouldn't you be in gaol?' When I left, he presented me with a silver keyring fashioned in the shape of a Roman wolf suckling the infants Romulus and Remus. Generously he explained the legend in detail. He wanted me to like Rome. He was a salesman for the eternal city.

Our second meeting was in Canberra. I was asked to take him to lunch. The lifts in the new Parliament House weren't working. Finally we climbed up the fire stairs to the dining room: harsh treatment for an ageing foreign minister. At lunch he swallowed six pills taken from different coloured bottles which he carried in his pockets. I wonder if there is a magic pill that will allow to him escape his web of criminal charges.

In Rome this time, I talked with a more astute observer than the gloomy barber about a nation's fantasies and images. She was less sensational than the Italian press. She had seen the film *GoodFellas* in a Roman cinema. The audience, she felt, were disgusted by it. *GoodFellas* was about corrupt politics and Mafia brutality. For years Italian self-perception has been clouded by the imagery of Hollywood films like *The Godfather*. Michael Corleone was, after all, a good family man, who knew precisely what a man had to do. He was almost likeable and, like Mussolini, Craxi, Andreotti and Berlusconi, he got things done.

It is an image, indeed a fantasy, totally inconsistent with the warmth and decency of the vast majority of Italians. Maybe, in the years ahead, they will get the politics off the front pages and settle for images of the things they do well, like fine suits and expensive cars.

Wannitwiflegs?

In the Italian city of Genoa there is a huge statue of Christopher Columbus, the discoverer of America. It is in a small park near the railway station. I stopped to look at it on an early morning walk. In the half light I noticed a mass of huddled shapes round the base of the statue. Looking more closely I saw that they were the sleeping figures of black Africans.

For a moment I wondered if it was some sort of demonstration: a subtle protest against the discovery of the New World, which had, with the help of African slaves, become the symbolic land of freedom and abundance. In fact they were just homeless people, stateless Africans, who had come to Italy illegally in search of a share of the relative wealth of Europe.

Illegal migration from Africa is a big problem for Italy. An estimated half a million a year cross the Mediterranean, destroying their passports or travel documents and refusing to say where they came from. Confronted with this technical statelessness the Italian authorities don't quite know what to do. They can't, they say, send them back. 'We don't know where they came from.'

It is not exclusively an Italian problem. Most European governments are confronted with similar situations—sometimes worse. The 'illegal' movement of people across traditional borders is becoming one of the great issues of our time. In Germany 'refugees' from Eastern Europe and the old Soviet Union, and guest workers from Turkey have provoked political division and the re-emergence of right-wing extremism. Foreigners have become targets for simple-minded skinheads. France and other European countries have similar difficulties.

Apart from recent efforts to tighten up on the procedures for admission of 'refugees', the Germans have in the last few years embarked on substantial infrastructure programs in Eastern Europe to create employment and raise standards of living. If, it is argued, things improve in the source countries then people will not be so attracted by the magnet of high standards of living in Germany. It is an implicit recognition that if law and order is to be maintained in the global village then the vast discrepancies between wealthy and poor countries have to be reduced. And this is not just a European problem. It was put another way to a friend of mine recently by a Chinese vice-president. 'The world,' he said bluntly, 'has a vested interest in the success of the Chinese government in implementing its policies and maintaining law and order in China. If we fail and 10 per cent of our population decides to leave, where do they go? That's 200 million people. Who will take them?'

Travelling to the United States I wondered how it, a nation built on mass migration, handled it all. At New York's La Guardia airport, I suffered a mild cultural shock, which for me seems an inevitable part of arriving in America. It was either the effects of overeating or a bit of a hangover which propelled me into the bar in search of some restorative elixir. I asked for a soda water.

'Wannitwiflegs?' said the barman. It sounded terrible, so I said I'd just have it normal. He planted a cardboard bucket about the size of a forty-four-gallon drum on the bar. I carried it gingerly to a nearby table and sat down to drown my discomfort.

Americans, it seems, do nothing by halves when it comes to

food and drink. They have the largest soda waters, the richest milkshakes and the thickest steaks. You have to find a pretty up-market restaurant to be served with the delicate portions made famous by French cuisine. The land of plenty is sometimes the land of too much. But the image of America as a bounteous country has over the centuries attracted the poor and oppressed. There's plenty to eat.

Struggling with my bucket of soda water, I recalled the Australian exporter of beach shorts which had to remake its range for the US market. Americans, I was told, have bigger bums than Australians. This, I thought at the time, is not a trivial statistic. It is appropriate for Australia, positioned between America and Asia, to have a compromise position on this issue.

I left the bar and hopped into a cab. 'Congratulations pal,' said the driver. 'You've picked the last cab in New York driven by an American.' For a few seconds I wondered what he meant. What is an American? Clearly the driver thought Blacks and Hispanics didn't qualify. He drawled on. 'Take me,' he said, 'I'm an American Jew and totally screwed up.'

'What are you screwed up about?' I asked.

'I'm an American Jew,' he replied. 'I'm supposed to be rich.'

This conversation took place a few miles from the Statue of Liberty. For over a century it has stood there at the gateway to New York and America. 'The mighty woman with a torch' has a message which symbolises American hopes and fantasies about a land of abundance and freedom, a refuge for the oppressed.

> Give me your tired, your poor,
> Your huddled masses yearning to breathe free,
> The wretched refuse of your teeming shore,
> Send these, the homeless, tempest-tost to me,
> I lift my lamp beside the golden door!

Half a mile from the Statue of Liberty, the former Immigration Reception Centre at Ellis Island has been turned into a museum. Like most historical museums it has a theme: in this case, hardship, struggle and ultimate success. Ellis Island is something of a shrine for the descendants of the millions of European migrants who were 'processed' there in the great waves of immigration at the turn of the century and in the 1920s. At Ellis Island you see the rooms where newly arrived migrants were hosed down, the prison-like dormitories in which they slept. They did it tough. At the museum cafeteria their prosperous goggle-eyed descendants marvel at it all, over king-size hamburgers and fish and chips. Even my disaffected cab driver told me proudly that his grandparents came to Ellis Island. And, in spite of the poignant memories of hardship and suffering evoked by the museum's exhibits, the success story is very apparent. European migration has been a huge contributor to American dynamism, and to the cultural and intellectual life of the country. The prosperous-looking visitors to the museum are a living tribute to a past which made America great.

Today the problem is that the beacon of the Statue of Liberty, originally pointed towards Europe, beckons to a wider audience. The 'tired', the 'poor', the 'huddled masses' are no longer in western Europe. They're in Africa, South America, parts of Asia. It's America's abundance which attracts them, more than the abstractions of liberty and equality. It does not matter to them that exaggerated notions of individual freedom have made America the most litigious country on earth, or that freedom includes the right to carry a gun.

A former United States senator and presidential aspirant told me that he feared the country had become ungovernable. 'In Los Angeles,' he kept saying, 'the Korean community has a well-equipped private army. How do you govern a country like that?'

The old rhetoric of abundance and freedom, however, lingers on. It is well understood by thousands of illegal migrants from South and Central America, and the Caribbean. And it is understood by Chinese 'refugees' who land from time to time on American beaches. They are, their representatives explain, 'human rights' refugees, who claim that the population policies of the Chinese government (limiting the number of children in each family) are inconsistent with their individual freedom. That is why they pay big money to be smuggled into America. If they prove their point, under current US immigration laws they have a fair chance of being accepted as refugees.

New York, of course, exemplifies the problem. It is the focal point of a great human experiment. Multi-ethnic, much-troubled, it exists on a knife edge of creative tension: it is a stew of human aspirations, eccentricity, racial tension, excitement, foibles and despair. Maybe my cab driver unconsciously summed up the human condition—and the problems of governments. 'What's your job?' he asked. 'You look like a doctor to me.'

'No,' I said, 'I'm not a doctor.'

He tried again. 'Maybe you're a crack dealer.'

'No, I'm not a crack dealer.' He thought for a moment. 'That means you're a businessman.' As I got out of the cab he smiled at me sadly and said, 'You know, my wife drives me insane, so I stay in the cab. It's been good to talk to you. I have a feeling I might pick up some weirdos later on tonight.'

A third generation American, he is also a child of New York, the microcosm of global problems of mass migration and urban living. He didn't sound entirely happy to me. But one feels his life could be far worse if the world's leaders fail to keep their nerve.

The City of Big Shoulders

'If you tell them you're from Australia they'll probably look at you to see if you've got a bone through your nose.' It was a warning which used to be given by an Australian friend who lived in America during the 1970s; a sort of psychological prophylactic to protect you from questions like, 'Where is it exactly now?' and 'Does everybody speak English down there?'

This sort of question is more likely on the East Coast of America. New York, for all its sophistication, must be one of the most self-absorbed cities on earth. San Francisco, on the other hand, is a good place for Australians to start if they want to be recognised and feel at home. More than any other city in America, San Francisco looks west across the Pacific. Thirty per cent of the population is Asian. It has a mild Pacific climate. Eating out at an Italian or Chinese restaurant, the people seem familiar. You could be in Carlton or Double Bay.

In a cab on the way to Fishermen's Wharf, the black driver asked, 'You're from Australia, aren't you?'

'Yes,' I said.

'I thought you were. Tell me,' he asked, 'have you read Manning Clark?' He seemed pleased that I had. 'Manning Clark wasn't the best of students at Oxford,' he said. 'But he went on to become an interesting historian. I've read his *History of Australia*. That Robert Hughes . . . he's more of an amateur, but he writes well. I liked *The Fatal Shore*.'

I asked the driver where he came from. He said he was born in Ethiopia, and went to school in Malta. His father had studied at Oxford at the same time as Manning Clark. He himself was a part-time student of international relations. Really he was a citizen of the world. San Francisco seemed a natural place for him to be.

It's hard to identify the average American, or a typical city in that country. It's not an easy place to define. 'America' is an ideal to which Americans are intensely loyal. In reality it's a collection of regions with separate economies and very different outlooks. California, and the Midwest, centred on Chicago, each have much larger economies than Australia's total economy. They're also quite different from each other. In lifestyle, San Francisco resembles Sydney. It embraces the water of San Francisco Bay, though less warmly than Sydney embraces its spectacular harbour. Chicago, like Melbourne, has an ambience of old wealth reflected in fine public buildings and great art collections. Melbourne's nineteenth-century wealth came from gold; Chicago's from cattle. Today San Francisco is about service industries, high tech and western seaboard trade. Chicago symbolises the American cult of bigness. The poet Carl Sandburg called it 'the city of big shoulders'. It has two of the world's tallest buildings, the largest grain market and the busiest airport. The Chicago Board of Trade is the world's biggest commodity market, the stock exchange the second largest in America. It also has other big statistics which are less well known. Forty per cent of the population is black. Half the adult black males are unemployed. Twenty per cent of the population is on welfare. One third of the black population lives below the federal government's poverty line.

I felt the ambience of the cult of bigness in Michael Jordan's Sports Bar in downtown Chicago. Jordan, the great basketball player, who also tried his hand at baseball and golf, is a multimillionaire. The bar is arranged in a tiered semi-circle, where the patrons sit, like bidders at a thoroughbred auction, facing a wall of huge television screens. One half of this electronic wall was showing the basketball finals, the other half the baseball. The clash of audio sensations and visual images was mind-boggling. The patrons roared their approval at the two screens, and sipped beer from containers which seemed the size of fire buckets. I touched my nose to see if it had a bone through it. At the back of the bar the great man's Nike basketball shoes were on display in a glass case. A small person, I gazed at them in awe. They looked like rubber boats, the sort of thing I could go white-water rafting in, down the Snowy River.

Americans delight in quantitative measurements and sheer size. When a friend asked a woman bartender at a restaurant bar, 'Is this a good seafood restaurant?' she replied by saying, 'This sir, is the fourteenth most profitable restaurant in the United States'—which seemed to be an answer to a different question. In a coffee shop where I asked for a 'small' cappuccino as distinct from a 'large' one, also on offer, it was served in a cup the size of a chamber pot. The imagery did nothing for the taste.

Americans are conspicuous consumers of electricity, gasoline, TV and food. There are more unhealthily fat-looking people in the United States than in any other country I've had the privilege of visiting. The cult of bigness extends to bags of popcorn, hot dogs and buckets of coke.

A sustaining myth is the belief in access. In theory any American can grow up to be president as, indeed, some of them have. Any American can create his own business and succeed. Those who don't tend to be regarded as people who have failed to take advantage of the opportunities available. So there is an underclass in a free labour market, which sometimes seems efficient and dynamic. Essentially it is a 'shoe-shine culture', attractive and reassuring to those having their shoes polished, but providing little comfort or dignity for the guy with the brush in his hand, who exists below the poverty line.

Australia has bouts of importing trends and gimmicks from the United States. So we have the world's biggest banana, the biggest pineapple, and some pompous skyscrapers. Melbourne's casino is the world's biggest. These choices are based on schoolboy politician imaginings of what tourists want. Tourists, in fact, are more discerning. Copycats leave them cold. Soon a lot of us will have pay TV. Lots of people will be disappointed when they see what they're paying for.

America, sadly, doesn't always export its best. It's hard to capture in images the vigour of the country, the old-fashioned charm and courtesy of 'middle' Americans and the warmth and rhythm of American blacks. The place is too big and diverse for impressions to tell the full story, and impressions can sometimes be unkind. I know. On my last day in Chicago I went to the art gallery. A sign above the reception desk said, 'Adults $6.50.' I handed the woman behind the counter $10.00. She gave me a warm smile and $6.50 change. I looked again at the signboard and read it more carefully: 'Adults $6.50. Social Security Cards and Seniors $3.50.' I gave the woman a forced smile and hobbled slowly up the stairs to look at one of the world's greatest collections of French Impressionist paintings.

The Place for a Village

I spread the copy of the *Sunday Age Sports Week* on the Brunswick-green tabletop so I could glance at it from time to time. The table was on the footpath outside a coffee bar in Lygon Street, Carlton. I was talking to my grandson, Harry. His parents were there too. *Sports Week* told me that the Sydney Swans looked menacing. *Che sera sera.* There was a smell of good coffee. The sun shone from a pale sky. Steam from the cappuccini loitered in the crisp air. It seemed a very nice place to be.

There were four people at a nearby table. I recognised two of them: Bob Ellis and Max Teichmann. Icons. Bon vivants, boulevard literati, epigrammatists drinking caffe latte. Ellis told me he was in town to see a memorable Melbourne Theatre Company production. I asked him what he thought about Lygon Street this beautiful Sunday morning. 'This,' he said, 'is a place where thoughtful people gather for discussions for the benefit of the entire nation.' He smiled whimsically, enjoying his own hyperbole.

Lygon Street is a good meeting place. It has the right mix of restaurants, bookshops, wine and coffee bars, cinemas, pubs and boutique shops. It's vibrant and has a bit of style. Fitzroy's Brunswick Street is similar, but also different. So is Chapel Street in Prahran, Ackland Street in St Kilda, Toorak Road in South Yarra, the footpaths opposite the town hall in Port Melbourne, and Bridge Road in Richmond. In different degrees they are each places of urban delight, where people congregate to enjoy themselves. There may be others. They're places which led an American visitor to say recently why he liked Melbourne. 'It is,' he said, 'unique. It has half a dozen Greenwich Villages.'

John Batman, the founder of Melbourne, scarcely leaps out of the history books as an attractive personality. He was too conspicuously upwardly mobile. As a young man he dobbed in his boss, who was subsequently hanged for stealing—an unusual abuse of the individual employment contract favoured by right-wing politicians. Later in life he displayed considerable skill in making and losing money. He was, however, a man of mixed talents and virtues. The first European settler to recognise Aboriginal land rights, he purported to buy them out with a doubtful contract and some gift-shop trinkets. But he saw the potential of Port Phillip, and founded a village which became a city.

Somehow, and some time after that, it seemed to go wrong. Melbourne's greatest physical disability is that it is back to front. The early civic fathers built a city on a classic grid pattern, and some great boulevards leading out of the grid. In the directions indicated by these first arterial roads, the wealthier settlers pushed out to Hawthorn, Kew and down to Brighton. Nowadays, St Kilda Road takes you to St Kilda Junction, and Sydney Road to the Sarah Sands Hotel. In spite of this, you can still see what the city planners had in mind. It was geometric, neat, and a touch European. But they turned the city away from the mouth of the Yarra, and Port Phillip Bay. The port became the tradesman's entrance: a sprawl of railway yards, warehouses and wharves, where few people lived and nobody wanted to go. Only in parts of Williamstown, where the astute sea captains built their houses, do you find that intriguing mixture of industry, housing and waterfront which provides a hint of what might have been if the city of Melbourne had embraced the bay.

Batman, of course, had confidence in the future and a touch of vision, qualities which have, like a bottle in the surf, emerged and receded in the civic history of Melbourne. According to some historians, Melbourne in the 1850s and 60s was the richest society in the world. I suppose you can only go downhill from there. Certainly the citizens of those days lacked nothing in confidence. They erected fine public buildings, including a great library, a parliament, and a treasury with underground vaults to keep the gold in. They had faith in an abundant future: like Alan Bond, Christopher Skase and John

Spalvins. In later moods of confidence, sometimes real and sometimes misplaced, and with a touch of vision, Melbourne was enriched with fine churches, the Exhibition Building, the MCG and the Tennis Centre.

In the early 1990s it became fashionable to say that what the place needed was confidence. But confidence can't be whistled up with the constant iteration of the idea that Melbourne people should see life as particularly miserable, a punishment for past excesses. And yet those, to borrow Joan Didion's phrase, 'who make and write the narrative of public life' seemed to believe it could be. And kept saying it. The rhetoric was confusing: like telling a boxer at the start of a world title fight, 'You're in terrible shape.'

The lack of confidence came from a recession, mixed up with an array of broad economic and social changes. Melbourne was not unique in this. The changes affected the whole country. New technology had a big impact. The idea of being part of a global economy seemed threatening. The world seemed out of sorts. Melbourne suffered additional bruises like the property boom and bust of the late 1980s, West Coast winning two Grand Finals, and the collapse of the State Bank. The city's traditional industries seemed in decline.

A more deep-seated anxiety is the suggestion that somehow Melbourne is slipping behind. Singapore with the same sized population has a better airport, better hotels and grows more rapidly. Melbourne is no longer the financial capital of Australia. Sydney has the 2000 Olympics. Brisbane surges ahead. There is a drift to the north, just as in the 1960s the Americans drifted to the south. Economically Melburnians may have to get used to the idea of being Australia's third city. All downhill from the 1850s. But dedication to catastrophe of this kind is an exercise in self-flagellation.

Rivalry between Sydney and Melboure has been long-standing and of some substance. It's been like a beauty contest to determine who looks better, richer and more sophisticated in the eyes of the world. In round one Sydney was the only entrant. As the site of the first settlement and the capital of the colony of New South Wales it represented European Australia. There was nothing else. It was responsible for the whole continent. So in 1803 an expedition was sent to Sorrento in Port Phillip Bay to protect the south from the possibility of French occupation. Port Phillip seemed a barren, inhospitable place and the little settlement was abandoned in 1804. Twenty years later Hume and Hovell walked from Sydney to Port Phillip and returned with a more favourable impression. In 1835 Batman and Fawkner settled on the Yarra River. It was the beginning of the city of Melbourne, part of the colony of New South Wales.

For some time the two settlements had little to do with each other. They were too far apart for easy communication. They had different lifelines to the mother country. But Sydney remained the official link with Britain until 1851 when Victoria became a separate colony. The separation from Sydney was the cause of great celebration. Picnics and sporting events were held in the shade of a gum tree called the Separation Tree. It still stands in the Melbourne Botanic Gardens.

The second round of the contest went to Melbourne. The discovery of gold swung the balance. It produced an economic boom, and the population of Victoria increased eightfold in ten years to a figure half as big again as New South Wales. Melbourne became the commercial capital. The city took on new pretensions. Collins Street became the best known Australian street, the boulevard of commercial power and a faintly European sophistication. For a while Sydney was even considered more respectable than Melbourne: a city whose charm derived from its interesting past. So with the federation of the six colonies Melbourne logically became the interim capital. Then Canberra was built—a foolish compromise between the rival aspirations of the two major cities.

Sydney in the nineties is the biggest financial centre in Australia. It houses the most hard-nosed businessmen. It is seen internationally as the epitome of the Australian way of life. It has the major gateway airport. It attracts more tourists and more international investment. It has the harbour, the powerful symbols of the bridge and the opera house, the ships nudging their way into the heart of the place. And at night the mixture of twinkling lights and water casts its own spell. This is the public face of Sydney which makes it the public face of Australia.

Worrying about the future of your own and other cities is, of course, a legitimate pastime. But it has its limitations. A few years ago a minister in the Irish government, sensing my own worries, counselled me in a kindly way to 'always remember, Senator, that posterity has never done anything for us'. But the Irish are a people of philosophic bent and unreliable as worriers. And there's not too much to worry about. The fact is that, for the vast majority of people, life in Melbourne is better than life in Moscow, Lagos, Manila, Tokyo, Los Angeles, or most other cities which come to mind. Nothing dramatic is likely to happen to change this situation.

More and more of the world's population is congregating in big cities. The important thing is to make them good places to live and work in. Increasingly the biggest cities are becoming poor environments, debilitated by traffic congestion, pollution, crime and lack of planning. Not all of them are like this. And some have compensating charms. Paris and Rome enjoy built environments of human scale and the richness of historical continuity. Venice has escaped the noise pollution of the automobile. Its buildings reflect history and are reflected in the water. New York is an exciting pot pourri of human foibles. Hanoi echoes a rich history of diverse cultures. Amsterdam has the magic mixture of old buildings and water. Seattle, Montreal and Melbourne have been described as the world's most livable cities. In Melbourne's case it has something to do with a proud past, good suburbs, public facilities, cafe life and sport. Melbourne people like all that. Sometimes they're afraid something will muck it up.

Not to muck it up is the challenge of Melbourne's next stage of development. There's room for differences of opinion and some optimism about the new exhibition centre, a planned new square for the city, a new museum, and a refurbished art gallery. Some good things are talked about, like specialist galleries to house the state's fine collection of Aboriginal art, and the Heidelberg collection. These things should build on Melbourne's strengths, enhancing its tourist potential, as a place with something different to offer. There are plans for infrastructure improvements to make the city work better. Public transport services should continue to improve. An accessible city will become livelier. And then there are some one-off 'big events'.

'Big events' are devised by the boys in the backroom who want to 'put Melbourne on the map' again. There's a fear they have a better eye for bread and circuses than for the things which make the city unique. Some of them are frantic about Melbourne's failure to attract the same number of overseas tourists as Sydney and Brisbane. The casino is the centrepiece of the tourist cargo cult. It is one of fourteen in Australia, and the biggest. It puts us ahead of the Joneses, but I don't think it does much for Melbourne's sense of difference. I can't see flocks of tourists descending on Melbourne in preference to Sydney, Brisbane or Perth because of the big casino. I can't see it making the city safer or providing more amenity for its citizens. Casinos come at a social price.

If you ask protagonists of Melbourne's big casino why we need one, you usually get an answer suggesting that a casino is the *sine qua non* of a civilised community. 'We've just got to have one,' they say, as if it were a pair of trousers or a sewerage system. Melbourne cannot be half naked or unfashionably noxious in a brave new world. Just occasionally they say it will increase state government revenues and create jobs. That's true, but the estimates are inevitably rubbery. And the same claims could be made for a telecommunications equipment plant or a food-processing factory.

Lloyd Williams, the chairman of Crown Casino, is bullish. Melbourne, he suggests, will become the beacon for gambling and entertainment, and an outstanding tourist destination, the Las Vegas of the southern hemisphere. I understand his interest, and his enthusiasm, but remain sceptical about his estimates, his ambitions for Melbourne, and his taste. I'm not keen on the idea of Melbourne emulating Las Vegas, Los Angeles, Bangkok, Singapore, or anywhere else.

Of course, in the late nineteenth century in Melbourne's heyday it was often referred to as the New York of the southern hemisphere. Since then New York has become a less livable city. Melbourne has moved slowly forward in fits and starts to become a city of some charm. It has half a dozen Greenwich Villages. New York has only one. They are worth looking after. And perhaps in its next phase of development the city can be turned round to face the bay.

Eureka!

We assembled, as instructed, at 10 a.m. on a roadway inside the main gates of the cemetery. At first there were about a dozen people. Every few minutes some more would arrive, and stand around talking in huddled groups. It was a cold, bleak morning. The drizzly rain came down at an angle, blown by the wind. It seemed to penetrate overcoats and jackets. People stamped their feet and blew on their hands. It was a typical Ballarat day.

By 10.30 the crowd had grown to about a hundred. A small group held a bedraggled banner inscribed 'Canadians for Eureka'. One man had a placard saying 'Californians Remember'; another a simple cardboard sign, 'In memory of Lt Ross'. Behind a nearby monument, marking a family grave, two men dressed in kilts and glengarries wailed away on bagpipes. Someone said, 'They're practising.' I approached a man who seemed to be in charge. 'What's happening?' I asked.

'Nothing yet,' he said. 'We're waiting for the Irish bus to

arrive from Melbourne. Should be here in about ten minutes. Can't start without the Irish.'

I decided to make use of the time and walked up a muddy path through crowded tombstones to my father's grave. I climbed onto the top of the grave and pulled a few small weeds from the surface, as my mother and I had done in years gone by. I suppose I went there out of respect and sadness. I respected him for what he'd made of his life from a poor start. The sadness came from the fact that I'd not known him very well. My father died when I was a teenager. Not always the best time in father-son relationships. He was a stern man. To me he seemed a distant figure. I think he wanted me to achieve things which I was incapable of. I suspect I disappointed him.

Ballarat was a good place to be as a child. We rode bikes (called 'grids') into the countryside to go rabbiting, played footy in the cold and mud, mucked about in cockleshell boats on the lake, and nervously explored the old goldmine tunnels. We gave that up when 'Pops' Dowling fell sixty feet down a mine shaft. A policeman got a medal for going down to get him out.

In the war years Mr Bromley, an Austrian Jewish refugee who ran the laundry round the corner from our house, was arrested as a spy. He had a noisy old washing machine. People who heard it thumping away during the night thought he was sending secret radio messages to the Germans. They reported him to the police. Mr Russo, our fruiterer, of Italian extraction, was also arrested for spying. He kept pigeons. People said he was sending messages to Germany. This caused a big drama. My father was very angry. It was the first time I heard words like 'bigots' and 'parochial nitwits'. He went to the Ballarat police station and kicked up a fuss. Mr Bromley and Mr Russo were released. I like to think my father had something to do with it.

I first heard the story of the Eureka Stockade from my dad. A very conservative mayor of Ballarat, elected on a 'Garden City' platform, and known as 'Begonia' Bartrop, decided to have a civic celebration to commemorate Eureka. He got in touch with the Eureka Youth League in Melbourne and asked them up to Ballarat for the opening event. He arranged to meet them in his mayoral robes at the entrance to the city. They arrived in a cavalcade of trucks decorated with red flags, and blown-up pictures of Lenin and Stalin. The mayor was very embarrassed. It was suggested he might have to stand down. My father thought this was very funny. I don't think many other people in Ballarat saw the joke. It was some years before I really understood it myself. In the meantime he told me all about the miners and the Eureka Stockade. It was a good time in our relationship. He took me to meet Mr Spielvogel, the secretary of the Ballarat Historical Society. Mr Spielvogel wore a wing collar, a bow tie, a waistcoat and a bowler hat. He had a musty office in Camp Street, cluttered with old books and papers. He spoke with a strange European accent, and looked at you over the top of his glasses, perched on the end of his nose. I was a bit scared of him. I imagined all historians must be like him and decided I didn't want to be one.

By the time I got back to the cemetery gates, the Irish bus had arrived. The doors opened, disgorging about thirty people dressed like extras in a film of an Irish county fair. They seemed a jovial lot. They had a sense of occasion about them. As if to prove the point, it stopped raining. A pale sun struggled out from behind the clouds. It seemed like the luck of the Irish.

This was in Ballarat on 3 December 1989. It was the 125th anniversary of the Eureka Stockade. I was there representing the commonwealth government, or more particularly the prime minister, Bob Hawke. There was no indication of what role I had to play. Did I have to make a speech? Just in case, I swotted up on the history of Eureka. For a Ballarat boy it was mother's milk. But I wanted to check on the details. I suspected there would be a number of experts present on such an historic occasion. The Eureka movement began with a build-up of goldminers' grievances against an incompetent and sometimes corrupt administration. It came to a head with police hunts to check on miners' licences, the acquittal on a charge of murder of a man called Bentley, and the burning down of the Eureka Hotel. As tension mounted, Governor Hotham, an out-of-touch bureaucrat, sent troops from Melbourne. The miners decided they would have to fight, and built a primitive stockade. A brief battle took place on 3 December 1854. Twenty-nine men were killed: twenty-four diggers and five soldiers.

It was an event marked by heady rhetoric on both sides. The miners were a multicultural lot, from various countries and embracing various political persuasions. Folk heroes were created. More importantly the diggers adopted the blue and white flag of the Southern Cross as the emblem of their struggle. Australia had foolishly avoided a war of independence. The Eureka Stockade was a Clayton's rebellion against authority, the best we could do. The flag lingered on as a symbol of solidarity and independence.

So 125 years later I stood in the crowd inside the cemetery gates, and wondered what would happen next. The man who'd said we had to wait for the Irish instructed us to form into a procession. The pipers took their place in the front, and the 'dignitaries', who included federal and state politicians, councillors and others, assembled behind them. The remainder fell into place at the rear. The procession, we were told, would march to the grave of the soldiers for a brief ceremony, and then on to the grave of the diggers. The pipers began to play. It sounded like they were still practising. The crowd, embracing a myriad of sentiments, shuffled off down a narrow roadway between the gravestones.

The soldiers' grave consisted of a plot half the size of a boxing ring surrounded by an iron picket fence. In the middle there was a granite obelisk. The surface of the ground was covered in gravel. A man called Seamus climbed over the fence. He said he was from the Connolly Association. He stood on the grave and patted the granite monolith with his hand. 'This monument,' he began, 'marks the resting place of the troopers killed at the battle of the Eureka Stockade.' He had a strong

Irish accent, an accent one could detect if he'd been speaking Chinese for a hundred years. He said that for a long time the diggers had been the heroes of the stockade. Historically the troopers had been ignored or reviled as tools of British imperialism, flunkeys of a colonial administration in Melbourne. But now, 125 years later, it was time for reconsideration, perhaps forgiveness. We should remember that 'some of the lads buried here were working-class boys caught up in events beyond their control'. It was another example of the contradictions of history. The crowd round the grave shuffled their feet. They were not quite sure what to think. They were relieved when it was announced that we would now march to the grave of the diggers.

At the diggers' monument I was invited to climb onto the top of the grave. This was a hazardous undertaking. The spikes on the iron pickets surrounding the grave were uncomfortably sharp. Finally I made it, and stood on the grave beside the obelisk while Seamus made another speech. He said that the diggers buried in the grave were heroes of mankind's struggle against tyrannical oppression. They were spiritual antecedents of those seeking the liberation of Ireland from the British. He mentioned similar struggles in Africa and America. Warming to his theme he moved closer to home. 'I ask you,' he said, 'what would the diggers think about contemporary politics in Australia?' He pointed to the ground beneath his feet. 'The men who lie here,' he announced, 'would turn in their graves at the high housing mortgage rates imposed on young couples in the outer suburbs of Melbourne by this rotten Hawke Labor government.' He raised the finger pointing to the ground, and turned it in my direction. I tried to put on my impassive look, and gazed over the crowd at the sombre horizon of gravestones. The sight of me seemed to encourage the speaker. The wages accord was a conspiracy between the government and reactionary trade union leaders to deny justice to ordinary wage earners. There were other injustices. At this stage he'd spoken for nearly fifteen minutes. The crowd was becoming restless.

'Get orf yourself Seamus,' a man shouted. There were intermittent boos. 'Shame, Seamus, Shame,' another interjected. The speaker began to wind down, and finally stopped. It was my turn.

I decided to be brief, statesmanlike, above politics. I'd speak about the Eureka Stockade. I began, however, with two fibs: whoppers in fact. 'It's a great pleasure,' I said, 'to be here on this historic Sunday morning.' That was one. 'I'm sure the prime minister would have liked to have been here.' That was the second. 'He's very interested in Australian history.' That took me back to the Eureka Stockade.

I finished my speech. Another man climbed over the picket fence and announced that he intended to speak. He said his name was Crowley. He informed us that he was a direct descendant of James Bentley, the owner of the Eureka Hotel, and the man acquitted of murdering a miner named Scobie. The hotel was burnt down by a bunch of 'conspiratorial' miners. The government of the day had promised compensation to those whose properties were destroyed in the riots. The compensation for the hotel was £29,000. It had never been paid. There had been a series of conspiracies against the Bentley family. James Bentley had been a victim of false and malicious rumours. Those who took part in the Eureka Stockade were a bunch of Irish radicals and other political extremists. The 'Irish connection' was still trying to use Eureka as a political platform.

For a few moments I thought I might be involved in a riot. 'What,' I asked, 'has all this got to do with me?'

Mr Crowley pointed a sheaf of papers in my direction. At the time of federation, he said, the new commonwealth government had agreed to take over the debts of the former colonies. Victoria had never paid the Bentley family compensation. The commonwealth was now responsible. The total now owing, including interest, was $36,545,000. 'Your government,' he said, 'should pay the bill.'

It seemed that it was time to bring the proceedings to a close.

'I think,' I said, 'that you should put your claim in writing. I'll refer it to the minister for finance.' Mr Crowley seemed slightly mollified. I climbed gingerly over the picket fence and mingled with the crowd. They seemed extraordinarily sensible and friendly. I left half an hour later. As I got into the car outside the cemetery gates the driver said to me, 'What went on in there?'

'Why do you ask?' I said.

'Well,' he replied, 'this Irish bloke came up to the car and asked me if I drove you. When I told him that I did he said, "We gave him a bit of curry in there today. But actually he's a bonzer little bloke."' We drove off and on the way back to Melbourne I tried to describe what had happened.

Mr Crowley accepted my invitation and wrote me a tightly written seven-page letter 'on behalf of all the Bentleys'. He finished the letter with the words 'God Save the Queen. Long Live Australia'. I passed the letter on to the minister for finance, Senator Walsh, with a covering note pointing out Mr Crowley's allegation that 'the Crown might try and get out of paying its debts'. Uncharacteristically Senator Walsh gave me a terse and unhelpful reply.

I met Seamus on one other occasion, as I went into a Melbourne reception for the visiting Irish President, Mrs Robinson. He was standing outside in the street, handing out leaflets. The leaflet said something about Mrs Robinson being a symbol of the reactionary state of Ireland. Her visit, it argued, should be boycotted. I stuffed the leaflet in my pocket. I like the Eureka flag, but I remain confused.

Afterlife

That's a Face I Know

THERE'S A slightly ambiguous phrase about being 'over the hill'. It has different shades of meaning. You can adjust it in your mind so that you're comfortable with it. Perhaps it means you've reached the top. The worst is behind you. It will be easier going from now on. More likely it means you've enjoyed the best of your life. You're worn out. From now on it's downhill all the way.

These judgments are highly subjective. You can adjust a bit here too. Perhaps you're really over the hill when the past looms larger than the future. At a certain point it's quite logical. There's more of the past. The future is increasingly about the next generation, children, grandchildren, hopes for posterity. The present is what you make it: hovering in the middle. The past is inescapable, like a ball and chain dragging behind you. The links in the chain go back to childhood. Ballarat is part of my past. So is politics.

People often ask me about life after politics. I was in Ballarat when I found myself contemplating the more important issue of death after politics, and how different countries arrange the 'after life' for their deceased political leaders. In Moscow, more than seventy years after his death, Lenin is still on display in his mausoleum. It is said that it costs fifty million dollars a year to preserve his body. A team of scientists works on it round the clock. It's hard to understand the point of it all. Looking at him in the mausoleum, you realise that he had no life after politics. He hung on to the end, dying in office. Perhaps that's the point. Poor Lenin. No 'life after', so he gets an expensive 'afterlife'. In his mausoleum in Beijing, Mao is the same. Thousands of people gawking at him every day—just like it used to be in the good old days. Will Lenin ultimately be removed from his mausoleum as a cost-cutting measure? Or because the system he created collapsed? Stalin was removed from the mausoleum when Khrushchev denounced him as a killing politician. Mao was a killing politician too. What will happen to his 'afterlife', as China rushes down the capitalist road?

Other countries prefer different images of immortality for former political leaders. In America there is an extraordinary sentiment about past presidents. When Nixon died most of America seemed to say, 'All is forgiven.' At the Arlington National Cemetery the superstars of the Kennedy era—Jack, Bobby and now Jacqueline—are buried side by side. The graves are a shrine for American pilgrims, re-creating in their minds the dazzling media legend of Camelot.

In Britain, the 'greatest' prime ministers finish up in Westminster Abbey. It's a big tourist attraction. The rest are scattered round the country. In Australia, there's no Westminster Abbey. Nothing like it. We could never agree on a site, let alone work out who is to pay for it. Melbourne has, however, in the familiar language of interstate rivalry, 'made a bid', with a prime ministers' memorial garden at the General Cemetery. I went to look at it one Sunday afternoon. Surrounded by a fence of spiked iron pickets, it's like Alcatraz, half adrift from the rest of the cemetery. The gate was locked. At some risk to my manhood, I climbed over the picket fence. At the entrance there is a small gazebo-like structure, not unlike a freshly painted outback bus station. It's a waiting room. The ashes of R. G. Menzies, 'the father of the Liberal Party', are buried in one corner of the garden, under a tombstone shaped like a giant coffin: the sort of thing which Boris Karloff might emerge from in a film about the 'living dead'. The garden is furnished with a small ornamental pool and a rustic timber bench where young Liberals might sit and reflect on their founder's wisdom. At the far end of the garden there's a large granite block, rectangular and upright, its surface chiselled into squares. The block is engraved with the names of every Australian prime minister, dead and alive. It looks like a filing cabinet, with a name and date on each drawer. At its base there are a few little jars containing dead flowers.

There's a sadness about this garden; not, one suspects, of the kind intended. I can't imagine anyone taking a foreign visitor to see it, even one from interstate. Half-hearted and too late, it's a bit of a compromise, perhaps even for Menzies, who on his first visit to Britain wrote in his dairy, 'At last we are in England: Our journey to Mecca has ended, and our minds abandoned to those reflections, which can so strangely move the souls of those who go home to the land they have never seen.' Maybe he would have preferred his memorial somewhere else.

Australians, generally, are not into monuments and shrines. Not many of us know where some of our most distinguished prime ministers—Deakin, Curtin, Chifley or, until recently, Menzies—are buried. Sensibly they became ordinary Australians when they left the political scene, their achievements documented in Hansard and the history books. In Ballarat, however, they are all brought together in the prime ministers' avenue of honour. It's a collection of the sculpted heads of all our prime ministers from Barton to Keating. Strolling into the Ballarat Botanical Gardens you pass the classical statue of a scantily clad maiden called 'Summer', and another more extensively robed called 'Spring'. Then comes Edmund

Barton, and Deakin, and the others in sequential order. The years of their prime ministerships are engraved on the stone column beneath each head. Only Gough has the date of his tenure in days and months, as well as years, inscribed on the column. It is as if to emphasise the grandeur of his rise and fall.

It's an extraordinary collection. They're all the same height. They have a stony look about them. One suspects they've all been to the same guillotine. Avenues of heads are a levelling experience, a guillotine for snipping tall poppies in the Australian manner. The avenue should be called BHOG: Ballarat Heads of Government. Standing in the crisp autumn air I thought of the terrible story of the terrorist who blew himself up with a bomb. There was not much left of him. His old mother, asked to identify the remains, stared closely at his head. 'It looks like him,' she said, 'but he was a much bigger man than this.'

Ballarat's heads of government was a nice idea at the time. It should be kept going, the avenue wandering on towards 'Spring' and 'Summer'. It's a place of interest when the rhododendrons lose their flowers. It's not without charm. But technology reduces the need for afterlife monuments, for mausoleums and granite slabs. Film and sound archives capture the substance of political lives better than any monuments. It's easier to judge what they were all about. They almost come to life.

I remember a meeting of the parliamentary Labor Party, just after an election. There was a ballot for the ministry. The returning officer made a speech instructing new members how to vote. 'You must,' he said, 'put a number in every square. There are no crosses here.'

'Only double crosses,' said a voice from the back of the room. It was Barry Jones. Everybody laughed—but nervously. Politics is always close to the edge. It brings out the best in human nature, and often the worst. It's sometimes funny. Like any job, it has its own set of skills. You meet all sorts of people and learn things from a range of experiences. It hones one's natural scepticism, setting you up for life after politics, a good time to study the human condition.

The question about 'life after politics' is a different one. I wonder who coined the phrase and stuck it into the popular imagination. You don't hear much talk about 'life after accountancy' or 'life after bus driving'. Politics seems to be different. Doctors sometimes pronounce on life after a heart attack or a hip replacement. How to cope after a traumatic experience. But politics is only moderate trauma. So when people ask, 'How's life after politics?', you sometimes wonder what they mean. It might be anything from, 'Are you enjoying yourself?' to 'What's it like being out of the limelight?' to 'Are you adjusted to release from the madhouse?' Each of these questions has some point to it, and tells you something about the questioner.

Three years is a short time out of politics. Leaving political life you walk through a glass wall into a different world. Behind you is a hothouse of feverish activity and arcane practices. Adjustments have to be made to accommodate the outside world: little things like rediscovering trams, opening your own mail, staying at home on Sunday nights, taking time to browse in bookshops and galleries. You discover new enemies: parking officers and drivers of Landcruisers, more threatening than the old ones left behind in politics.

Outside the hothouse, life is relatively anonymous, with some exceptions. 'That's a face I know,' a man said recently, as we waited at the pedestrian lights. He peered at me closely, rummaging in his memory. 'I know who you are,' he announced triumphantly, 'you're an actor, a television actor.'

'Not any more,' I said. 'That was a while ago now.'

He gave me a sympathetic look. 'I'm sorry about that,' he said. 'I know acting is a tough game.'

The lights turned to green. Our conversation was exhausted. So we smiled at each other and diverged as we crossed the road, an out of work actor, and an ageing television junkie.